Sex, love & you

Making the Right Decision

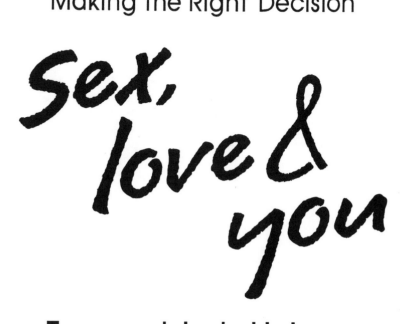

Sex, love & you

Tom and Judy Lickona
with William Boudreau, M.D.
Photography by Chad Weckler

AVE MARIA PRESS
Notre Dame, Indiana 46556

Thomas Lickona, Ph.D. has been in forefront of the movement for the formation of good character. He was a participant in the 1994 White House Conference on Character Building for a Democratic Civil Society; his book Educating for Character: How Our Schools Can Teach Respect and Responsibility received the 1992 Christopher Award; and he serves on the Board of Directors of the Character Education Partnership, a national coalition working to promote character development in schools and communities. Lickona, a husband, father, developmental psychologist, and Professor of Education at the State University of New York at Cortland, is also the author of *Raising Good Children* (Bantam Books).

Judith Lickona is a mother and homemaker. She has also been a college teacher. She and husband Thomas speak together to teenagers and their parents on the subjects of sex, faith, and morality. They have also taught religious instruction to teens in their parish, Saint Mary's Catholic Church, in Cortland, New York.

William J. Boudreau, M.D., is a family physician who sees young people as part of his medical practice. Drawing on his fifteen years of experience as a doctor, he speaks to teens and young adults on the dangers of sexually transmitted diseases. He is married to Alanna Boudreau. They have five children.

Chad Weckler is a professional photographer in New York City.

To Saint Joseph

Letter addressed to Ann Landers taken from *Ann Landers* column. Permission granted by Ann Landers and Creators Syndicate.

Letter addressed to Dear Abby taken from a *Dear Abby* column by Abigail VanBuren. Copyright 1968. Distributed by *Universal Press Syndicate*. Reprinted with permission. All rights reserved.

Scripture quotations contained herein are from the New Revised Standard Version Bible, Catholic Edition, copyright 1993 and 1989, by the Division of Christian Education of the National Council of Churches of Christ in the USA. Used by permission. All rights reserved.

International Standard Book Number: 0-87793-540-8

Library of Congress Catalog Card Number: 94-71887

Cover and text design by Elizabeth J. French

Photographs: Copyright © by Chad Weckler.

Printed and bound in the United States of America.

Acknowledgments

We would like to thank …

… Mike Amodei, our editor at Ave Maria Press, for the many things he did to make this a better book. We feel blessed to have had an editor who was a real partner on this book.

… Frank Cunningham, director of publishing at Ave Maria, for his enthusiastic support of the book and the helpful editorial direction along the way.

… the many chastity educators who are helping young people realize the benefits of saving sex for marriage; their work has been an inspiration to us.

… our parents, Win and Ed Lickona and Tom and Mary Barker, for raising us in the Catholic faith.

… our children, Mark and Matthew, for helping us to know the joy of raising a family.

… the sisters of the Third Order of St. Francis, the Sisters of Mercy of Albany, New York, and the Sisters of St. Joseph of Carondolet, for Judith's Catholic education.

… Bill and Alanna Boudreau, for their friendship, their contributions to this book, and their commitment to promoting the virtue of chastity.

… the students—Joe Beauchamp, Rachel Lieberman, Mike Bonagura, Melissa Dovi, Hugo Cardona, Grace Cohen, La-Channa Sumpter, Donnell Cooke, and Eun Gyeong Hwang—from Cortland College Collegians for Life and B.A.S.I.C. (Brothers and Sisters in Christ), who were photographed and contributed thoughts to the chapters, "How Can I Be Chaste?". We would also like to thank Christy Cobler, Colleen Chapman, and Rory Gilhooley who are also featured in the photographs.

… Jack Danileson's Restaraunt, Cortland, New York, and the Caleion Room of the State University of New York at Cortland, for permitting us to shoot photos on their premises.

… Robin Straus, our agent, for her unflagging support at every stage of the book.

… The Lord and our Blessed Mother, who we feel certain led us to Ave Maria Press, made this book much more than we had envisioned, and brought it to fruition in God's time.

Contents

Introduction

Ten years ago when our younger son Matthew was in sixth grade, he came home from school one day and told us that many of the boys in his class had started to "go with" girls. What did this mean? Well, a few weeks later he said that several of the same boys told him that they were going to have sex with these girls once they got into seventh grade.

A bunch of pre-adolescent boasting, right? Unfortunately, statistics show that this kind of talk isn't always just talk. Each year the average age of the first sexual activity for boys and girls gets younger.

What was going on? When our sons were growing up (Matthew is now 21, his brother Mark is 27) we were very clear about what we expected of them. In the area of sexuality, we expected them to remain virgins until they married (if marriage was what God called them to). We asked this of them because we were concerned for their own happiness. We wanted them to live the life God intended for them.

Incidents like the one Matthew experienced at school helped us to see clearly the difficulty our sons and their peers would face in making the choice to remain chaste.

As they went through school, we witnessed first-hand how the moral environment—especially the sexual environment—was changing.

One big change occurred in the media. For example, in the 1970s, the television heroes and heroines—the lawyers, detectives, doctors, and police officers—began to be portrayed as engaging in and condoning casual and uncommitted sex. An average one-hour soap opera contained at least one sex scene between unmarried partners.

Motion pictures were even more graphic; nudity and sex scenes—often accompanied by foul language and violence—filled the screens. By the early 80s these films were into our homes on cable television. Soon after you could rent them at your local video store.

Popular music directed to a teenage and pre-teen audience also promoted sex. Songs with titles like "Go All the Way," "Take Your Time (And Do It Right)," and "I Want Your Sex" moved onto the charts. Cable television again provided a place where the lyrics could be illustrated visually.

In short, it was a world turned upside down; values that would make you truly happy—like honesty, unselfishness, and sexual purity—were ridiculed, called puritanical, or, at the least, declared impossible to live by.

The residue of this so-called "sexual revolution" is what your generation—unfortunately—has inherited. Growing up preoccupied with sex, many boys and girls do begin to experiment with sex even before they reach puberty. The results? Teen pregnancy, sexually transmitted diseases (now, including the deadly AIDS virus), regret, and guilt are among the unhappy consequences of this premature sexual involvement.

Thankfully, in spite of the onslaught of destructive messages, both of our sons grew up and made the value of chastity their own. We truly thank God for this.

Then, about six years ago, we were asked to share our views on sex at a public high school assembly. We addressed both young men and young women in our presentation.

We told the young men never to let anyone tell them that virginity isn't manly. We said that a man who has control over himself, who has his ideals, and who respects women as much as he respects himself, is indeed a real man.

We told the young women to not believe the popular opinion that equates virginity with being immature or repressed. The truth, we said, is that real maturity and real affirmation of your sexuality means being able to wait for the unique relationship—marriage—in which sexual love is a secure and joyful expression of a man and woman's total commitment to each other.

We don't know how many young people went away agreeing with what we had to say, but it was easy to tell that they had listened.

Since then we have given this talk about sexuality many times, sometimes just to young people, sometimes to young people and their parents together. Then we began to write it down. Eventually, our message became the content of this book that you are about to read.

Along the way we became friends with Dr. William Boudreau, a family physician. He has an in-depth knowledge of sexually transmitted diseases (STDs). He has treated many young people who have contracted an STD. We think you will be interested in what he says about the physical dangers associated with premarital sex.

We hope you'll open your mind and heart to what we'd like to share with you.

God bless you and keep you. We hope you know how much God loves you. We will pray for you.

TOM AND JUDITH LICKONA
Cortland, New York
April, 1994

Part 1

Distinguishing Between Myth and Fact

I was 15 the first time. I had heard so much about it. You know, the girls whisper on the street, in the locker room and everything, and the boys make dirty jokes. It was supposed to be something wonderful, and it wasn't. I just felt, "Well, it's over. Big deal."

... A lot of guys think that if you're going to have a girlfriend, then sex goes along with that. I don't think that way anymore.[1]

—a 17-year-old girl

I don't want a girl who will tease me. I'm saving myself for my wife, and I hope she waits, too.

—a 17-year-old boy

As a young person, you are in a crucial period of your life. You're laying the foundation for your future. The decisions you make during these years will affect your life for years to come. Sex is one of the things you'll have to make a decision about. Right now you likely belong to one of the following four groups:

1. You have never had sexual intercourse, and you do not intend to do so until you get married.

2. You have never had sexual intercourse, but you're not sure what you think about sex before marriage.

3. You have had a premarital sexual relationship, and you don't see anything wrong with it.

4. You have had a premarital sexual relationship, but you now consider it a mistake, and you plan to wait until you are married before you have sex again.

No matter which group you belong to, it's difficult to make the right decision about sex. How *do* you decide? Some people say, "Trust your own feelings." Other people just say, "Don't," period. Parents and teachers might tell you one thing, friends something else.

We hope that what we say will be relevant to you, regardless of which of these groups you're in. If you have not already had sexual intercourse it is very likely that you will have a chance to do so in the near future. You'll find yourself with a person who will let you know that he or she will permit you to have that experience. You're going to have to decide between now and then what you are going to do when that moment comes.

In this section we'd like to distinguish between some myths and facts commonly associated with the issue of young people and sex. We will examine three questions that you may have heard someone ask about sex, or you may have asked yourself.

Chapter 1, "Isn't Everybody Doing It?" provides you with up-to-date statistical information about what it means to be sexually active and the number of teens who fall into that category. In chapter 2, "Why Are Some People My Age Choosing Sex?" you will be presented with a list of thirteen reasons that may—in one combination or another—influence your decision to have or not to have sex. Some of these reasons—for example, sexual attraction, parental permissiveness, and loneliness—are not anyone's fault, rather they just **are**, and it's important to be aware of them. Finally, many teens and unmarried young adults associate sexual activity with "how it feels." According to that logic, "If it feels right, do it." Chapter 3 looks at the difference between making decisions based solely on feelings and making decisions with our minds.

We hope that by introducing these facts—some of which may be new to you—and by pointing out myths, you will be able to make a much more informed decision about sex.

Chapter 1

Isn't Everybody Doing It?

At a suburban high school near Los Angeles, police recently arrested ten male students on suspicion of rape and "lewd conduct." According to news reports these students all belonged to a club called "Spur Posse," whose members competed to see how many girls they could have sex with.

The district attorney eventually decided not to press charges when it appeared that all of the girls these boys had slept with had consented.

One female student interviewed by a reporter said that students at the school had absorbed the message that "having sex is a normal part of adolescent life."

Stories like these seem to lend support to what you may have heard some people say about sex: *Everybody's doing it.*

The truth, however, is otherwise: Everybody is *not* doing it.

According to a Lou Harris public opinion poll, only 28% of all students in junior and senior high school combined say they have had sexual intercourse.[1]

In senior high school, nearly half of all students say they are still virgins, according to a 1992 report by the Centers for Disease Control's Division of Adolescent and School Health.[2] Among students in grades nine to twelve, 52% of girls and nearly 40% of guys say they have never had sexual intercourse.

It's also important to know that, according to the latest research, only 39% of high school students are *currently* sexually active.[3] In some earlier surveys of sexual behavior, a person who had sexual intercourse just once in the past was misleadingly described as "sexually active" and lumped in the same category of with other people who may have had intercourse many times. According to one analysis, 20% of "sexually experienced" teenagers aged 15 to 17 have had intercourse only once.[4] Many of these teens stop having sex after their first sexual encounter.

What are some factors affecting whether a person decides to be sexually active or remain a virgin?

Sexual activity rates are lower for young people who are high achievers. For example, 73% of teenagers chosen for a recent edition of *Who's Who Among American High School Students* said they have never had sexual intercourse.

Religion is another influential factor. In a 1987 Associated Press report, among 12- to 17-year-olds who said they "attend religious services frequently," only 18% say they had had sexual intercourse. By contrast, 38% of the same age group who said they "seldom or never" attend religious services reported having had sexual intercourse.

Environment also plays a role. Adolescent sexual activity rates tend to be much higher in poor urban areas. Also, sexual activity is higher among youth from single-parent homes.

In 1993 the Salt Lake City *Institute for Research and Evaluation* published a research report titled "Predicting and Changing Teenage Sexual Activity Rates."[5] It identified several important factors that predict which teenagers are likely to become sexually involved.

One factor identified by the study was the young person's sexual values. If teens agreed with statements such as, "There are lots of advantages to saving sex for marriage" and disagreed with statements such as, "It's natural to have sex with someone you like," then they were much less likely to get sexually involved.

Another important factor is friends. The study found that a teenager with friends who supported abstaining from sex was more likely to remain a virgin until marriage than someone who did not have friends who supported this belief.

Drinking and drugs also played a big role. Teens who never drank were the least likely to have had sex. For teens who got drunk just once, however, the probability of sexual involvement increased considerably. Those surveyed who had gotten drunk within the past week were highly likely to be sexually active. Sexual activity and drug use followed a similar pattern.

Most popularly reported statistics on teenage sex don't give these kinds of detailed breakdowns relating sexual activity to other beliefs and behaviors. As a result, a false impression is created and made known that all groups of young people are equally sexually active.

If You're Waiting, You're Not Alone

What all these statistics tell us is that if you're a virgin, you're not alone. In fact, you have plenty of company—including lots of young people who are clear about their values, take their faith seriously, have set goals for themselves, and are working hard to achieve them.

These findings also tell us that if you're not a virgin you can stop sexual activity and find plenty of people who support that choice. We'll say more later in the book about making a new commitment to chastity—often called "secondary virginity." But we want to emphasize here that you can make the decision to start leading a chaste life right now. You can't regain your physical virginity, but you *can* regain your chastity.

Chapter 2

Why Are Some People My Age Choosing Sex?

There are lots of reasons why some people your age make the decision to get involved in sex. It's likely that a combination of reasons have influenced their choice. Listed below are some of the possible reasons. You may be able to add others to the list.

1. *Sexual attraction.* Human beings are sexual creatures; we are sexually interested in and attracted to others. Sexual intercourse is essential to the survival of the human race. The power of sexual attraction is one obvious reason why some young people get sexually involved.

That's not to say, of course, that sexual desire *compels* anyone to have sex. Hormones aren't destiny. Human beings have a God-given free will and are capable of controlling even strong desires.

And the sex drive, strong though it can be, is not like other biological drives—such as the need for food and water—which are related to personal survival. Kathleen Sullivan, director of *Project Respect*, puts it this way: "Nobody's ever died from not having sex. It's the one appetite that's not necessary to fulfill."

For many young people, sexual desire does get stronger—and harder to control—once they have gotten sexually involved. Guys generally tend to fall in this category. However, this isn't always true. For many other people, especially young women, the first sexual experience is disappointing. "Take my word for it girls," says one 16-year-old, "sex does not live up to the glowing reports and hype you see in the movies."

2. *Societal and media pressure.* Popular opinion says, "Go for it!" We live in a sex-saturated society. Advertisers use sex to sell things. Popular songs promote sex.

We see sex on TV. Soap operas, for example, show or discuss sex between unmarried partners at least once an episode.[1] Talk shows endlessly discuss sex—usually sex outside marriage. We see sex graphically portrayed on the movie screen between characters who barely know each other.

One recent R-rated movie included fourteen instances of sexual intercourse between unmarried people. In another popular movie, the "heroine" suggests to the guy that they have sex on the first date, explaining that she prefers it that way.

Everywhere the message seems to be: "Sex is the center of the universe. You need sex to be happy. Sex is an essential part of any dating relationship."

Obviously, not all young people who see sex portrayed in this way are going to run right out and do it. But we're kidding ourselves if we think that a media-centered world in which sex dominates cannot have any influence on us. We are creatures of our social environment. What we take in stays in our mind—our unconscious mind, if not our conscious awareness.

Eventually, the constant bombardment of sexual messages and sexual stimuli can weaken our defenses and make us more susceptible to sexual temptation.

A young married couple we know, Theresa and John, were able to wait until after they were married to have sex. But it wasn't always easy. When Theresa looks back, she recalls situations that she and John put themselves in that increased their temptations:

We were both committed to waiting until we were married. But it can be hard when you already have strong feelings, and then you go to the movies and the people up on the screen are doing what you look forward to doing with the person you love.

Says another girl, who lost her virginity as a high school sophomore: "At fifteen, I began dating an older guy. One night we went to see a very sexy R-rated movie. On the way home,

SEX, LOVE, AND YOU

we took a detour and had intercourse in the back seat. Five months later, he broke up with me. I was crushed."[2]

Maybe this guy and girl would have had sex that night even if they hadn't seen the R-rated movie. But it's reasonable to assume that media stimuli do influence, consciously or unconsciously, our readiness to engage in sexual activity.

3. Peer pressure. The need to belong, to feel accepted, is a deep human need. From adolescence through young adulthood there is an especially strong desire to feel accepted by one's peers. That need can make it hard to resist peer pressure to do things that are not good for us—to drink, do drugs, or get involved in sex.

The Harris poll asked sexually active teenagers, "What factors influenced you to first have sexual intercourse?" Peer pressure was the primary reason.[3]

A few years ago, *Newsweek* magazine ran a cover story on teenagers and sex. It began with a quote from a girl they called Mary, who was 15 years old. She said:

I was part of a group in junior high school that was into partying, hanging out, and drinking. I started to have sex with my boyfriend, and it was a real downer. It was totally against what I was, but it was important to be part of a group. Everybody was having sex. I couldn't handle the pressure.[4]

Says a 15-year-old boy: "If a guy lets it be known he's a virgin, other guys will laugh at him, tease him. It's a peer pressure thing, an ego thing."

4. Pressure from a partner. Some young people can handle peer-group pressure but find it a lot harder to handle pressure from a person they're involved with—and really like. Listen to what a high school girl says about the pressure she's getting from her boyfriend:

I really enjoy being with Jack. I feel so happy when I'm with him. We make out a lot, and as time goes on we've spent less and less time talking and more and more making out.

Now he wants to go all the way. I don't think I really want to. Last weekend on our date he even cried because he loves me more than anything and he wants to "show me" in a real way. I love him, too, but I don't want to do it. What can I say?[5]

The pressure doesn't always come from the guy. More and more often, it comes from girls.

Says one 17-year-old girl: "Guys have trouble dealing with girls who come on to them. They don't want word to get around school that they refused." Says an 18-year-old boy: "It ain't cool for a guy to tell a girl no."

Guys in this situation may feel their manhood is on the line. They don't want to look like a prude or have their sexuality challenged.

5. *The desire to be "normal."* Recently, we were at a high school outside San Francisco doing a workshop for teachers. During the lunch break one of the teachers spoke to us and shared her concern about all the sexual activity going on among students at her school. She told us:

In the last few years, many kids have gotten it into their heads that they should have sex by the time they are 16. They think there is something wrong with them if they haven't had this experience by this age.

Said a girl at another high school: "If you don't have sex, you're not going to grow up right."

We saw in the last chapter that everybody is *not* doing it. In fact, most high school students are not currently sexually active. But if young people are under the false impression that everybody *is* doing it, their human desire to be "normal" may lead them into sexual activity.

SEX, LOVE, AND YOU

6. *Parental example and permissiveness.* For some
teenagers, what goes on in their own homes may influence
them to get involved in early sex. Says one high school boy
who lives with his father: "What's the big deal? A lot of my
dad's girlfriends spend the night." A 15-year-old observes her
mother's dating habits and says to herself, "Mom's doing it—
why shouldn't I?"

Sometimes parents, by what they allow their children to do,
send them the message that they wouldn't disapprove if they
had sex. Two mothers of teenage daughters were talking about
the upcoming senior prom. The first mother said: "My husband and I are so relieved! The dance is at the hotel, the parties after the dance are at the hotel, and then the kids all have
rooms at the hotel for the night."

The second mother swallowed hard and said, "But don't
you realize what signal that sends to kids—what it gives them
permission to do?"

The first mother sighed and said, "Well, at least they're not
drinking and driving."

The second mother who told of this conversation later
commented: "As parents we draw a line, and then we cross
it. We draw another line, and then we cross that. Pretty soon
we've compromised our moral standards to the point of
disappearing."

7. *The wrong kind of sex education.* Sometimes the sex
education students get in school is long on information (facts
about reproduction, AIDS, contraception, etc.) but short on
moral values (such as self-respect and respect for others) and
reasons to avoid premature sexual activity. The school comes
across as being value-neutral on the matter of sexual intercourse.

The school's approach to sex education may also send a
mixed message: "Don't have sex (you could get pregnant or
catch a sexually transmitted disease), but here's a way to do it
fairly safely (use a condom)."

Says a high school boy at the California school that had the
Spur Posse club: "They pass out condoms, teach sex education

and pregnancy-this and pregnancy-that. But they don't teach us any rules."

A senior at another high school comments: "No one says not to do it, so by default they're condoning it."

8. *Mistaken beliefs.* Have you heard any of the following?

"You can't get pregnant if you do it standing up."

"You won't get pregnant if you're drunk when you have sex."

"You're safe if you do it near the time of your period."

"Douching afterwards prevents pregnancy."

"Taking the pill will keep you from getting a sexually transmitted disease."

"Washing after sex reduces the chances of AIDS infection."

All of these statements are false. But surveys of teenagers find that many believe and then act upon these popular misconceptions about sex.

9. *"Don't know what else to do."* In the South Bronx, New York, the pregnancy rate is 180 per 1,000 girls each year, nearly twice the national rate. So a community agency sponsored an essay contest. The topic: "How Can the Problem of Teenage Pregnancy Be Solved?"

One of the five high school finalists wrote that teens are more sexually active today partly because they are "bored." They have "nothing better to do." Lack of opportunities for constructive teen activities—especially in poverty-stricken areas—increases the likelihood that teenagers will be sexually active.

10. *Drinking and drugs.* A lot of young people, unfortunately, equate good times with drinking. Alcohol is a sedative drug that affects the central nervous system. It reduces inhibitions and affects judgments. Behavior a person would normally find unacceptable when sober is harder to avoid after drinking. The first sexual experience of many teens happens after they have been drinking alcohol.

The combination of alcohol and other drugs—besides being potentially deadly—is even more capable of obliterating inhibitions and causing young people to do things that may be totally out of character. A 17-year-old wrote to an advice columnist to describe how that happened to her.

Four couples, all good friends, decided to spend New Year's Eve together. One of the guys had the house to himself; his parents were out of town.

First there was great music, great dancing. Then someone brought out liquor. People began smoking pot. At midnight, someone suggested strip poker. By then, all inhibitions were gone. Promiscuous sex soon followed.

"I've been miserable and depressed ever since," wrote this young woman. "Crummy, immoral behavior is against everything I believe in." But drugs and alcohol were powerful enough to wash away those beliefs for the moment and lead her to act in ways completely contrary to her normal self.

11. Low self-esteem. Studies show that young people with low self-esteem—those who are the *least* mature and confident—are more likely to get involved in sex at an early age.[6] They use sexual involvement as a kind of security blanket that makes them feel wanted, grown-up, or part of the group.

It's sad but true that some young people have so little self-esteem that they feel that sex is the main thing that makes them attractive to other people. Says one 16-year-old girl: "I've been sexually active, if that's what you want to call it, since I was in fourth grade. The first time I did it was with my cousin. I've tried it with a lot of guys. It makes me feel wanted. You know, I have something that somebody really wants."

Another teenage girl who got pregnant and is now an unmarried mother says: "My brothers and their girlfriends said that if you didn't do it, you were a nerd. I had always been sort of an outcast, and I didn't want to be called a nerd, so I got involved in sex."

12. Loneliness. A few years ago *Psychology Today* did a survey on loneliness. Of the 42,000 readers who responded, two-thirds described themselves as feeling lonely. The percentage was even higher among high school students who answered the survey.

What do people often do when they feel lonely? They try to get close to somebody. Sex is one way to try to do that. Some people use sex to try to cement a relationship that would otherwise not last.

For the same reason, some girls have sex because they want to get pregnant. They want a baby because they want someone to love and love them back. There's an emptiness in their lives that they're trying to fill up (and they have sex in their attempt to do it).

13. *No good reasons to say no.* A 21-one-year-old college student said:

Chastity has been an enormous challenge for me during my college years. I have failed at it because I couldn't answer the question, "Why shouldn't I have sex?" I gave in because I figured, since I didn't have a solid answer, I must be wrong. I also read all this stuff that claims that virginity is unnatural, abnormal, and "repressed."[7]

A lot of young people, unfortunately, are like this young woman. They haven't heard any or enough good reasons for saying no to sex before marriage, and so they end up getting sexually involved.

This chapter has presented you with thirteen reasons why some young people are drawn into sex. Try to remember these reasons the next time you wonder, "If it's such a big mistake for kids my age to get involved in sex, how come so many do?"

Chapter 3

Can Something That Feels Right Be Wrong?

Do you know about the "law of diminishing returns"? The law of diminishing returns is simple: It says, the more you do something, the less satisfying it is. This law can apply to sexual behavior.

For example: If you're a guy and you're dating a girl you really like, those first kisses are pretty exciting. But as time goes on, the level of excitement goes down; just plain old kissing doesn't do it anymore. You need to do something different to get the excitement level back up.

So you try French kissing. That works for a while, but eventually the law of diminishing returns takes over and open-mouthed kissing isn't what it used to be either. You need something new.

So you get into petting. But before long, conquering the same old territory isn't as much fun as it used to be. What used to be satisfying just isn't satisfying anymore. So you go all the way.

There's only one problem. When you go all the way, that's all there is. There isn't any more. What do you do when *that* starts to lose its excitement? Maybe you find a new partner, somebody more exciting to you. And the cycle starts again.

Notice that at every step of the way in this process, feelings—sexual feelings—have been in the driver's seat. Not moral judgment. Not respect for self or the other person. Not foresight and concern for long-range consequences. Certainly not love.

Feelings are important. But as Mike and Rita Marker, authors of the pamphlet *No Is a Love Word*, put it: "Feelings can't tell you whether something is right or wrong. They can only tell you how something feels."[1]

We've all done things that were influenced by strong feelings, things that felt right at the time—but which we thought differently about later on.

A decision—especially an important one about whether or not to have sex—is something you should make with your mind, not your feelings.

> *Our main reproductive organ is our brain. That's where the reproductive decisions are made.*
> *—Molly Kelly*

Dick Purnell, a counselor who has written several books on relationships, sexuality, and values, often speaks about what happens when we allow our sexual feelings to direct our behavior. We heard Dick Purnell speak recently to a college audience. His topic was "Sex and the Search for Intimacy," and he had an overflow audience of college students and other young people who wanted to hear what he had to say.[2]

He began by saying that we all have a deep desire for intimacy. We all want to really know someone and be known by them. We want someone to be close to us.

But, Dick Purnell pointed out, it takes a long time to really get to know someone. You have to do a lot of communicating to find out what another person is really like.

For example, questions you may ask when getting to know others are:

How do their emotions work?

How do they react to different situations?

What makes them feel angry or sad or depressed?

What makes them feel good about themselves?

How do they think?

What are their opinions about things?

How do they make decisions?

What is their concept of God?

Do they even think there is a God?

What are their values?

What do they understand to be their purpose in life?

When you know these things about a person, you have an intellectual, emotional, and spiritual intimacy—the kind that produces real closeness.

But most people don't go after this kind of intimacy. Sadly, a lot of people don't even know that this kind of intimacy exists; it's not even on their mental screen. Their notion of intimacy is the one society projects: sexual intimacy.

But there's a problem, Purnell said, in pursuing an intimacy that's based on sexual feelings. That's the problem that rears itself in the law of diminishing returns.

People don't talk out loud about the hurt and the guilt and the emptiness that comes from this pattern of sexual behavior. But as a counselor, Dick Purnell says he hears about it over and over: "People come to me, and in the privacy of my office they pour out their hearts and talk about the emotional scars that fill their lives."

Other counselors hear similar things. Says psychologist Dr. Henry Brandt:

Frequently, I listen to young men and women who have had experiences with heavy petting or premarital sex relations. They describe a similar pattern. They say, "First, there was great pleasure in it. Then I started hating myself. Next, I found myself hating my partner. We ended up embarrassed and ashamed. Then we broke up and became enemies.[3]

We think we want sex, Purnell adds. But what we really want is not sex. What we really want is intimacy. Knowing somebody else and being known by them. Valuing someone for the person they are and being valued in return. Sex outside marriage is not the way to get that.

Part 2

True Love Waits: The Dangers of Premarital Sex

At a conference in Ontario, Canada we took part in a discussion group for parents of adolescents. One mother described a problem she was struggling with:

> My daughter Susan is 15, almost 16. About a year ago, she met a boy, Dave, at the church youth group. He was nearly three years older. They began dating steadily.
>
> Recently, Susan came to me and said, "Mom, Dave and I feel we are ready to have sex."
>
> I was stunned. I said to her, "But, Susan, sex is meant for love."
>
> She said, "But we *do* love each other, and this is the way we want to express it."

The mother drew a deep breath and concluded her story, "At that point, I didn't know what to say to her."

We suggested to this mother that one thing she could do is ask her daughter what she means when she says that she and her boyfriend "love each other." What does it really mean to "love" another person? How do you know when someone really loves you? Consider this definition of love from a pamphlet put out by the Christian Action Council:

Love Waits

Love is patient ... Love starts with being friends—with taking time to get to know each other. It's sharing the good and bad times together.

Love is kind ... Love wants to do the best thing for another person. It's doing thoughtful things for someone else. Love never demands something that will harm you or the person you love.

Love will never cross the line between what's right and wrong ... It's right to care about someone. It's wrong to put one another in danger of having to deal with hard choices ... choices that could change both your lives, your goals and plans forever. Having sex before marriage may feel right for the moment. But the possible costs of an unexpected pregnancy, abortion, and sexually transmitted diseases—as well as the deep hurts that can come from a broken relationship—outweigh the feelings of the moment. The feelings are temporary; their consequences are long-lasting.

Love waits ... All good things are worth waiting for. Waiting to have sex until marriage is a mature decision to control your desires. Waiting allows you to build strong friendships ... to treat yourself and others as unique and valuable individuals ... and to treat sex as something exciting and special to be shared with one person for a lifetime. If you are getting to know some-one—or are in a relationship—remember: If it's love, love waits.[1]

In other words, to love another person means *wanting what's best* for the other person. A person who wants the best for you is concerned for your welfare, your happiness. Not just your welfare and happiness in this moment, but for your future as well. Love also means loving yourself enough to do what is best for you.

The question, then, for the mother to ask her daughter, for the girlfriend to ask her boyfriend, for you to ask yourself, is whether or not having premarital sex is really an act of love. *Is premarital sex really what's best for me and the other person?*

One way to answer that question is to consider the harmful consequences for self and other that premarital sexual involvement can bring. In this section we will examine three such consequences: *pregnancy, sexually transmitted diseases, and emotional and spiritual hurts.* Are these consequences fruits of a loving relationship?

If someone wants what's really best for a person he or she loves, sexual involvement outside a committed relationship clearly fails the test. If you're gambling with someone's happiness, future, and life, you can hardly claim to love them.

So when somebody puts pressure on you to have sex by saying, "If you love me, you will," you can truthfully reply: "If *you* loved *me*, you wouldn't ask."

Chapter 4

How Would Pregnancy Affect My Life?

Outside of marriage, the discovery of pregnancy can be a ter-rifying experience. It's as if the rest of your life has been put on hold; the pregnancy clouds every waking thought, every decision. A girl's reaction is often one of shock:

"I can't believe I'm pregnant."

"This can't be happening to me."

"I can't tell my parents—my father will kill me."

For the boy, finding out that his girlfriend is pregnant can cause similar confusion and panic:

"What is my responsibility?"

"How do I know it's my child?"

"I'm too young to get married. What about my plans for the future?"

The suffering caused by teenage pregnancy takes many forms.

For example, every year about 500,000 girls run away from home—nearly half of them because they are pregnant. One reason they run away is that they were afraid to tell their parents. (That in itself is a tragedy; hopefully it is clear to you that your parents will love you no matter what you do and that in a case like this you could go to them for help.) Many of these runaways go to big cities and eventually get trapped in prostitution.

Only a minority of school-age girls who get pregnant finish high school.

Pregnancy is reported to be the leading reason for suicide among teenage girls.

Less than half of the teenage girls who get pregnant marry the father, and those who do are twice as likely as any other group to get divorced.

Each year about 300,000 thousand babies are born to unmarried teenage mothers. Most children in this situation grow up without a father. Fatherless families produce disproportionate numbers of adolescents who do drugs, get in trouble with the law, drop out of school, or get pregnant themselves. In 1960 only one child out of twenty was born to an unwed mother. Now one in four children are born into a single-parent living situation.[1]

What Are the Options?

When an unmarried couple conceives a child four options are open to them.

Option one is to get married. Marriages that begin with a pregnancy can succeed. It depends on a lot of factors, especially support from others. We know a young woman who became pregnant when she was a junior in college. She and her boyfriend had been going together for nearly two years. They loved each other and believed that getting married was the right decision. Their families were very supportive both before and after the marriage. Ten years later, this couple is happily married and the parents of four children.

More often, however, marriages that begin because of a pregnancy fail. Sometimes the decision to marry is not made freely. There may be lingering resentment of the so-called "shotgun" nature of the marriage. The couple may not be mature enough to take on the responsibilities of marriage and parenting.

A second option is to give the baby up for adoption.
Only a generation ago, when there was less social acceptance for being an unmarried mother, about 95% of unwed mothers chose this option.

Adoption is a loving choice. There are thousands of married couples waiting to adopt a child. There are even waiting lists of people wanting to adopt babies with severe medical problems. These couples are prepared to handle the full range of responsibilities of parenthood. They are willing to love the baby as they would their own natural child.

This is not to say that giving up a baby for adoption is easy for the birth mother; it is very hard emotionally for a woman to let go of the child she has brought into the world. But knowing that the baby has been given a loving home is something a she can feel good about and take pride in for her entire life. And giving up a baby for adoption is a much wiser choice for a woman than trying to raise a baby when she is not adequately prepared.

A third option is to keep the baby and raise it as a single parent.   These days this is a common choice, but it is nevertheless one that should not be made lightly because of the many difficulties that are ahead.

If you talk to people who are parents, they will likely tell you that parenting is probably the hardest thing they've ever done—and that's true even when there are *two* parents to share the work and back each other up. When the whole job of parenting falls on one person's shoulders, it can be overwhelming.

Single-parent mothers are also very likely to be poor and to remain in poverty indefinitely. They struggle to keep food on the table and to pay all of the bills. They struggle against loneliness, frustration, and depression.

Children in this situation are often the victims of child abuse. The babies of teenage mothers are more likely to have emotional problems and to be held back in school. There are, of course, exceptions to this pattern. But, generally, being a single parent—especially if you are a teenager—is not a situation conducive to your happiness or your baby's welfare.

A few years ago *Time* magazine ran a cover story titled "Children Having Children." It profiled 15-year-old Angela whose experience of single-parenthood is not uncommon:

Angela finds it hard to think of herself as a mother. "I'm still as young as I was," she insists. "I haven't grown up any faster." Indeed, sitting in her parents' living room, she is the typical adolescent, lobbying her parents for permission to attend a rock concert, asking if she can have a pet dog, and complaining that she is not allowed to do anything.

The weight of new responsibilities is just beginning to sink in. "Last night I couldn't get my homework done," she laments with a toss of her blond curls. "I kept feeding him and feeding him. Whenever you lay him down, he wants to get picked up."

In retrospect she admits, "Babies are a big step. I should have thought more about it."[2]

The fourth option of a couple facing an unmarried pregnancy is abortion. Abortion sometimes seems like the easiest way out of a premarital pregnancy. Upon hearing that you're pregnant, friends may say to you, "Why don't you just get an abortion?" Others may offer, "I can help you pay for it."

If you're a girl who is pregnant, you may feel pressure to abort from your boyfriend. He may threaten to leave you if you don't get an abortion. (Usually, after the girl does get the abortion, the boyfriend ends the relationship anyway.) In some cases, a girl may face pressure to abort from her parents or other family members.

Because abortion is legal and common—about one-third of the nation's annual 1.5 million abortions are performed on teenagers—many young people choose this course. They typically do so without knowing the facts about prenatal development (how a baby develops in the womb), about what the abortion procedure does to the developing baby, and about the medical and psychological risks of abortion for the woman.

Abortion is a momentous decision that has life and death implications—not only for the developing baby but for the mother as well. It is vitally important for anyone considering an abortion to be informed not only about what abortion does to the baby but also about the physical and psychological risks for the mother. In some states (unfortunately, to date only a few), there is now a law that requires a doctor to provide this information to the woman so that she can make an informed medical decision. What follows is a summary of some of these important issues—both physical and psychological—that are crucial for anyone considering an abortion to know about.

Medical Risks of Abortion for the Mother and Developing Child

By Dr. William Boudreau

How the Mother Is At Risk

Abortion involves a definite medical risk for the mother. Typically, these risks are not explained to women thinking about having an abortion. Some of these risks include:

1. Bleeding. Not uncommonly, a woman suffers heavy bleeding after an abortion. The later in the pregnancy the woman has the abortion, the greater the risk of excessive bleeding. The loss of blood may be enough to require a blood transfusion.

2. Infection. Removing the baby and placenta by abortion leaves a raw surface inside the woman's womb that can easily become infected. The instruments used for the abortion can carry germs inside to this raw surface or to the fallopian tubes. Antibiotics are given to the woman most of the time to try to reduce infection risks.

3. Uterine Perforation. The sharp instruments used to remove the baby can sometimes put a hole in, or "perforate," the womb. This can lead to serious internal bleeding and infection, and damage other organs like the intestines. Major surgery may be needed to repair the damage.

4. Cervical injury. The forceful opening or "dilating" of the woman's cervix to remove the baby may cause permanent damage in the form of weakening or scarring. Sharp instruments or the boney fragments of the dismembered baby may also tear and injure the cervix.

5. Death. Each year in the United States, a small but significant number of young women die from complications due to abortion.

6. Later problems. Having an abortion increases the likelihood of difficulties in a later pregnancy. These risks include higher rates for miscarriage, tubal pregnancy, having a premature or low birth weight baby, and having a deformed child. Infants born to mothers who have had a previous abortion have a two to four times greater than normal chance of early death.[3]

Abortion also increases a woman's risk of becoming infertile. And recent studies have linked a greater chance of developing breast cancer later in life with women who have had an abortion.

The Facts of Prenatal Development

While abortion brings serious medical risks to the woman, the risks to the preborn child are more definite: abortion means death. In order to understand such a claim, it's important for you to understand how a baby develops in the womb. It's important to view human life in a long spectrum that includes childhood, teen years, adulthood, middle age, old age, and death. This pathway does not start at birth, however, but at the moment of conception.

At the moment the mother's egg and the father's sperm unite, new life is created. Here are some other scientific facts about life in the womb:

■ Even before the fertilized egg attaches itself to the mother's womb (within 4 to 8 days from conception), the baby's sex has been determined.

■ The baby's blood cells are present at 17 days. As early as 18 days, the baby's heart is beating and pumping its own blood supply (different from the mother's).

■ Eyes start to form at 19 days.

- In the third week of pregnancy, the foundation of the brain, spinal cord, and entire nervous system have been established. In the fourth to fifth week, the small unborn child looks distinctly human, yet the child's mother still may not know that she is pregnant.

- By the sixth week, the baby's brain waves can be measured.

- By the ninth to tenth week, the baby can squint, swallow, move his or her tongue, and make a tight fist.

By the eighth week, every major organ and body part is present that will be found in a full-term baby. From the eighth week of pregnancy until a person has reached adulthood, further changes in the body will be mainly in growth and in fine-tuning the body's working parts.

You are basically the same person you were inside your mother's womb—just different in body dimensions and refinements in how your body works.

Five Common Abortion Procedures and What They Do

The result of an abortion is that the live baby is killed and removed from its mother's womb. As is the case for the mother, the procedure is not a simple and smooth one for the baby either. The following are five abortion procedures used at different stages of pregnancy:

1. Suction and Curettage. This type of abortion is most common in weeks 7 through 12 of the pregnancy. A hollow tube with a knife-like edge is inserted into the woman's womb. A powerful vacuum is attached to the tube, and the baby is then cut into small pieces and sucked into a jar.

2. *Dilation and Evacuation.* Known as D&E, this procedure is generally performed after 12 weeks when the baby is too large and the skeleton too hard to be sucked out by a tube. The abortionist must reach into the womb with a knife-like instrument in order to kill the baby. A pliers-like device is used to crush the skull and spine and remove the baby from the womb.

3. *Saline Abortion.* Sometimes called "salt poisoning," this type of abortion is done in weeks 16 to 24 of the pregnancy. A needle is passed through the woman's stomach wall and into the womb, and a highly concentrated salt solution is injected. The salt surrounds the baby's body, and is also swallowed by the baby. Over the course of an hour the baby is burned, scalded, and poisoned before dying. The mother delivers a dead baby, usually within the next 24 hours.

4. *Prostaglandin Abortion.* This method, used after the fourteenth week, involves a hormone either injected or applied to the cervix. The hormone precipitates a continuous labor contraction that empties any baby, no matter what size, from the mother's womb. The labor forces may be so violent that some babies have their heads sheered off as they are expelled. Occasionally, babies are delivered alive during abortions performed using this method.

5. *Dilation and Extraction.* The abortionist uses an instrument to twist the baby about so it can be pulled from the womb feet first. The D&X method is typically used after the fourteenth week of pregnancy. The baby's head, the largest part, stops at the narrow opening of the womb (cervix). A blunt scissors-like instrument is jabbed into the base of the baby's skull, and the baby's brains are removed. The head collapses, and the dead body is then pulled from the womb.

Psychological Risks of Abortion

Besides the medical risks connected with abortion, many psychological aftereffects of abortion are often overlooked.

Post Abortion Syndrome (PAS) is the name given to the psychological problems that are associated with symptoms like guilt, sense of loss, bad dreams, and flashbacks for women who have had an abortion. Post Abortion Syndrome may not be experienced until months or years after the woman has had the abortion. Says Beth, a dental hygienist who had an abortion when she was in college, "It happened to me when I was giving birth to my first son five years later. That triggered the memory of the abortion. I saw what could have been."

The *Washington Times* interviewed Nancyjo Mann, founder of a group known as WEBA (Women Exploited by Abortion), a national support group for "women who hurt—physically, emotionally, mentally, and spiritually—from abortion."

Nancyjo Mann spoke first of her own abortion, a saline abortion performed on her when she was five-and-a-half months pregnant: "I liked me, Nancyjo, prior to the abortion. But shame and remorse and guilt set in. It's not something you go around telling people, that you just killed your baby. I was ashamed, totally ashamed."

The interviewer then asked Nancyjo whether or not she considered her feelings to be characteristic of other women who have had abortions. She answered:

My case is not unusual at all. I'm sure there are women out there who are never fazed, never, by their abortion. But I would say that 98% of them are fazed, whether it's for a small period of time or for the rest of their lives.

Some of the other characteristics of PAS are mourning, regret, remorse, suicidal impulses and other self-destructive behavior, loss of confidence, lowered self-esteem, anger, rage, and a preoccupation with death. Nancyjo Mann added:

There is a desire to remember the death date. A preoccupation with the would-be due date or due month. My daughter was due in early March.

There is an interest in babies, but a thwarted maternal instinct. We have many women in our group who cannot hold children. There's a hatred for anyone connected with abortion. A lack of desire to enter into a relationship with a partner, a loss of interest in sex, and an inability to forgive oneself. Nightmares, seizures and tremors, feelings of being exploited. And child abuse. We see a lot of child abuse.[4]

Researchers and counselors debate what percentage of women experience PAS. Some contend that only a minority do. However a study by David Reardon, the author of *Aborted Women: Silent No More*, estimates that as many of 8 of 10 women who have had abortions are at risk for PAS.

Men, too, can suffer from the emotional aftermath of abortion. Chris Flattery of Manhattan Pregnancy Services runs one of the few clinics that counsel men with PAS. One of his clients, a New York City radiologist, tried in vain to stop his girlfriend from getting an abortion. He is still angry and depressed with the feeling that he failed to protect his child.

If you have had an abortion, or know of someone who has, spiritual healing is available from a Catholic-sponsored group called Project Rachel. Explains Barbara Thorp, the Project Rachel director in the Boston area:

Our priests and counselors are trained to deal with what a woman has gone through physically, the violence enacted on her body. Second, they deal with the emotional trauma, such as unresolved guilt. Third, they focus on the spiritual repercussions of having an abortion and on ministering God's forgiveness.[5]

What to Do If You Are Pregnant

If you are now facing a crisis pregnancy, or face one in the future, we'd like to offer this heartfelt advice:

Take a deep breath. And take the long view.

Pregnancy lasts nine months, not forever. If you can't take care of your baby there are many people who would count it a great blessing to have that opportunity. You will bring much happiness to their lives if you offer your baby for them to adopt. And you will not be destroying God's most precious gift of human life.

If you discover you are pregnant (or, if you are a guy and your girlfriend is pregnant), remember: Your life won't be the same as you foresaw before the pregnancy. But with God's help it will be a better life for all concerned. What has happened is not ideal, but every experience enriches us, and the difficult experiences often teach us the most valuable lessons.

You will be okay. The crisis will pass, and you will go on.

If you think you may be pregnant, or are currently facing a crisis pregnancy, you can call these toll-free numbers 24 hours a day for helpful and compassionate counseling, pregnancy testing, prenatal care services, information about adoption, and other support services:

The Nurturing Network   **1-800-TNN-4MOM**

Birthright   **1-800-848-LOVE**

Bethany Ministries   **1-800-BETHANY**

If you have had an abortion and would like counseling and healing, you can inquire at a local Catholic church about Project Rachel, or contact their headquarters to find an office near you:

Project Rachel
National Office of Post Abortion Reconciliation and Healing
3501 South Lake Drive
Milwaukee, WI 53207
1-800-5-WECARE

Chapter 5

Why Is Premarital Sex a Danger to My Physical Health?

By William J. Boudreau, M.D.

We have all witnessed political revolutions in our world in recent times. Consider the upheaval of the former Soviet Union, the eastern European communist bloc, and the constant turmoil of numerous regimes in Africa. Typically, epidemics of disease, starvation, or violence follow on the heels of revolution.

In a similar way, society's revolution of attitudes toward sexual relationships, birth control, pregnancy, and marriage over the last 30 years has triggered its own epidemic of consequences. Known originally as the "sexual revolution," it has caused definite and significant risks for those who have chosen to participate in it.

One of the epidemics spawned by the sexual revolution is sexually transmitted diseases (STDs). Among sexually active young people, only the common cold virus causes a higher percentage of illness. There are more than 33,000 thousand new cases of sexually transmitted infections each day. Teenagers are the most susceptible to becoming infected.

In my 15 years as a family doctor I have seen many young people as patients who have unfortunately become infected with an STD. They are upset to learn that their symptoms are caused by a sexually transmitted infection. Recently, for example, 17-year-old "Andy" came to me worried about a burning sensation he was having when urinating. He had also noticed a slight amount of mucus-like discharge from his penis. After doing a sensitive test, I explained to Andy that he had contracted chlamydia, one of the STDs that is increasingly common among sexually active single people his age.

"Mary," age 18, came to me for a complete check-up, including a pelvic examination and Pap smear. A Pap smear is a screening test for problems of the cervix (tip of the womb). Mary's Pap smear revealed that she had been infected by HPV (human papillomavirus), which may be the most common STD in young people. This was very distressing news to her.

Very often, my young patients are not only distressed but also quite surprised to learn that they have contracted one of these sexually transmitted diseases. Often, they had never even heard about the disease they now have—what it is, the problems it causes, how it's transmitted. Or if they did know about it, they didn't think they could get it if they practiced "safe sex" by using a condom. (I'll explain more in chapter 7 about why condoms provide little protection against most STDs.)

In this chapter, I'd like to tell you the medical facts I think you need to know about the six most common STDs among unmarried, sexually active young people. There are actually about 40 different types of sexually transmitted infections, but we'll focus here on the ones that are most worrisome. First, some general points that are true of all these sexually transmitted diseases:

- The infective agents causing STDs generally live only in the human body, and do not survive outside the body.

- The spread of STDs occurs through sexual intercourse or other genital contact (such as oral sex). STDs can also be spread to the developing baby during pregnancy in an infected mother, or to a baby at the time of birth.

- In general, girls are more at risk than boys of getting an STD. And once they have contracted a disease, girls suffer much greater negative health effects than boys. STDs such as HPV (human papillomavirus) and chlamydia infect delicate female structures like the cervix and/or the fallopian tubes. Infections caused by STDs can result in cervical cancer, infertility, or complications if a girl is later able to get pregnant.

Here is a closer look at each of the six sexually transmitted diseases that pose the most serious health threat to young people:

1. *Human Papillomavirus (HPV)*.   Human papillomavirus, or HPV, may be *the* most common STD today. Studies reported in the *American Journal of Diseases of Children* (December, 1989) find that up to 38% of sexually active teenage girls have been infected. Even more recently, fully 46% of women students going to the gynecology clinic at the University of California at Berkeley were found to be infected with HPV.[1]

The rate of infection for this particular STD is likely as high for boys as it is for girls, but girls seek medical care for HPV more frequently. That makes tallying up the percentage of male infection more difficult.

What health problems does HPV cause? First, genital warts. In males, the wart-causing virus can infect several areas: the penis, the inside of the urinary tube (urethra), the scrotum, the anal area, and inside the rectum.

Females may become infected externally on the vulva and in the anal area, as well as internally on the vaginal walls, the cervix, and inside the rectum.

When visible HPV warts do occur, they appear as soft, slightly pale or skin-colored finger-like projections on the genitals. They are often small (3-5 millimeters), though left untreated, they may become sizable (as big as a walnut, sometimes even as big as an orange). Warts may cause some itchiness or irritation, and sometimes bleed.

HPV warts, however, can also be quite sneaky. Generally, they cause no visible symptoms at all. A lot of people infected with HPV have "sub-clinical" or hidden infection, and no growths on their genitals can be seen.

Often, when I am examining a patient for genital warts, I can detect them only after I soak the genital area with an acidic stain, and then use a magnified light for examination.

So, a big problem with HPV is that *most people infected with it don't know it.*

Aside from the unpleasantness of these wart-like growths on one's genitals, HPV carries with it a much greater danger. HPV-infected tissues develop a much higher risk of becoming cancerous. The first sign of this worrisome development often is an abnormal Pap smear that shows pre-cancerous or actual cancerous change.

Any woman who has become sexually involved, no matter what her age, should have a yearly Pap smear done as part of an examination of the reproductive organs. The Pap smear is performed by gently scraping the cervical surface and canal with a narrow brush and a spatula. Sometimes, pre-cancer change, or actual cancer, is found on the first Pap smear if there has been a delay of a few years between the start of sexual activity and the examination.

Cervical cancer generally develops slowly, over several years. Pap smears can detect very early "pre-cancer" changes that are fairly easily treated.

Some people, however, develop these pre-cancer changes more quickly. If you are a teenage girl, you are the *most* susceptible of any age group to the cancer-related effects of HPV. That's because the tip of your womb, or cervix, has a very sensitive area of cells, or "transformation zone." This is a particularly vulnerable area—one that the human papillomavirus attacks, causing changes or transformations in these cells that can lead to cancer.

Left undetected, and untreated, cervical cancer will become invasive and spread to other areas of the body. About 7,000 women in the United States die of cervical cancer each year. *Cervical cancer does not occur in girls who remain virgins.* It is directly related to infection by human papillomavirus (HPV).

In my own practice, I have encountered many young women suffering serious consequences of HPV. "Kathy," age 22, came to my office for an annual exam and Pap smear. She'd been sexually active since the age of 16. Her Pap smear revealed advanced pre-cancerous changes. Kathy described herself as "scared stiff" when I told her about the findings. She had an aunt who had recently undergone major surgery and radiotherapy for invasive cervical cancer.

Fortunately, Kathy's cervical disease was curable, using an electric wire loop to cut away a thin layer of the infected, pre-cancerous tissues. It was disturbing for Kathy to know her condition had been due to a sexually transmitted disease.

Besides cervical cancer, HPV can also lead to cancer of the penis, the anus, and the vulva (vaginal lips), though those occurrences are more rare.

Treatment of HPV. HPV is a tough bug to treat. As I mentioned, a person generally needs to be "stained up" with an acidic formula in order for all the infected areas to be seen. Once visible, the infected areas can be treated by a variety of caustic chemicals, by freezing, by electrically burning, by cutting, or by using a type of laser.

Follow-up treatment is routinely needed because hidden areas are not always detected at first. It may take many treatments to finally eliminate a virus that simply does not seem to want to go away.

2. Chlamydia. Chlamydia rivals HPV in occurrence. The true number of chlamydia infections is difficult to accurately determine, since tests to detect the chlamydia germ are not uniform. Also, many states do not have laws requiring doctors to report chlamydia infections to the public health department. A recent study places the number of chalamydia infections at four to eight times the number of HPV infections.[2]

The younger you are, the greater your risk of infection by chlamydia. The risk for females is multiplied because of the sensitive transformation zone of the cervix, the same area that is so vulnerable to HPV.

Chlamydia is sneaky, like HPV, in that the majority of infected people don't have a clue that they are infected.

Chlamydiae are delicate bacteria that typically infect the surface-lining cells of the urinary tube (urethra) or the woman's cervix and cervical canal. Young women infected by chlamydia may develop urethritis—an irritation of the urinary tube—and feel an urge to urinate frequently, usually with some discomfort. Young men who do get chlamydia symptoms most commonly have urethritis as well. This irritation causes a pain and burning sensation during urination and sometimes a bit of noxious discharge from the penis. Most of the time, however, as with HPV, no symptoms occur.

The most serious problem related to chlamydia is *the threat it poses to a young woman's ability to conceive a child later in life.*

Chlamydia may first infect the woman's cervix and cervical canal. Generally, no symptoms develop with infection at this site. But there is a significant risk that the chlamydia infection will travel up higher through the cervix canal—to the womb and the fallopian tubes. The fallopian tubes are vital in getting pregnant, because a woman's egg must travel down through a tube on its way to being fertilized by the man's sperm.

When the chlamydia organisms reach the woman's fallopian tubes, pelvic inflammatory disease (PID), or infection of the tubes, occurs. When a woman's tubes become inflamed in this way, scarring may happen, and this scarring narrows or blocks the passageway through the tubes. This narrowing or blockage may make it difficult, or even impossible, for a woman to get pregnant later on in life.

Teenage girls have a *10 times* higher risk of developing PID than older women. PID produces definite symptoms, particularly pain low in the abdomen, and sometimes fever. These symptoms may be serious enough to require hospitalization.

The tragedy and suffering caused by chlamydia-triggered PID are tremendous. After just one PID infection, a girl has as high as a 25% likelihood of becoming sterile; after a second infection, a 50% chance; and after a third infection, as high as a 75% probability of being unable to get pregnant.

You may not be aware of this, but right now one of every six newly married couples in the United States is having difficulty conceiving a child, frequently because of the leftover scarring of the woman's tubes from pelvic inflammatory disease.

There's still another serious danger. For a woman who has had PID and then later does become pregnant, there is a dramatically increased risk of ectopic or tubal pregnancy. In a tubal pregnancy, the newly developing embryo gets trapped in a scarred tube and begins to grow in that abnormal location.

If undetected, this embryo will grow and rupture through the fallopian tube. Massive internal bleeding can occur, and emergency surgery is needed. Ruptured tubal pregnancy is a significant cause of death. Deaths of teenage girls because of these tubal pregnancies have increased 400% since 1970.

Treatment of Chlamydia. When discovered in the early stages (urethral or cervical infection), chlamydia can be relatively easy to treat with antibiotics. Unfortunately, many infected women don't come for help early because they have no symptoms. The later complication of tubal scarring is extremely difficult to treat, and usually leaves permanent damage.

3. Herpes. The herpes virus occurs in two common strains, Herpes Type 1 (the cold-sore virus) and Herpes Type 2 (genital herpes). Herpes Type 2 is the most common cause of genital sores or ulcers. In the United States, one out of six sexually active men and women are estimated to be infected with the genital herpes virus (20 to 30 million people).[3]

Though commonly associated with unsightly genital sores or ulcers, most people with genital herpes infection, and who are capable of spreading it, do not even know they have it. This is because most people with Herpes Type 2 do not develop *visible* sores and are therefore unaware of their infection. Like the sneaky HPV and chlamydia viruses, a person can "pass around" herpes without even realizing it.

A smaller percentage of individuals exposed to the virus do develop genital sores and ulcers. These blistery sores do cause plenty of physical and psychological pain.

For example, severe pain can develop in an infected person's genital area, along with fever and flu-like symptoms. The groin glands often become enlarged and tender. Crops of blistery sores or ulcers scatter over the genitals. It may take up to three weeks for these sores to heal. Some people are more susceptible to a serious illness developing after their first contact with genital herpes. Occasionally, the illness is so severe that hospital care may be needed.

A vexing problem for people who do have herpes symptoms is recurrent episodes. After the first painful episode settles down, repeat episodes follow, sometimes monthly or every few months. Though not so severe or long-lasting as the first outbreak, these later occasions are nonetheless distressing. Many infected people become discouraged over these recurrences. Feelings of depression, anger, and guilt are common.

"Vicky," age 17, is one of several young people who go for counseling to help them cope with sexually transmitted diseases they have contracted. Vicky has genital herpes. She got it the first time she had sex, when she was 15. Now, almost monthly, her menstrual cycle triggers the outbreak of the herpes blisters. She has to cope with this suffering on top of all the normal stresses and strains that young people face.

A true danger also exists for babies at the time of their birth if the mother is experiencing an outbreak of herpes. The baby may become infected with herpes as it passes through the cervix and vagina during the delivery. The herpes virus can then invade the baby's nervous system and cause death or irreversible brain damage. If you have herpes and are pregnant or become pregnant, *you must tell your doctor.* Your baby's life may depend on it.

Treatment of Herpes.   An anti-viral drug is available for treatment of herpes infections. The drug interferes with multiplication of the virus and thereby reduces symptoms and the frequency of recurrences, but it is not a cure. Unfortunately, once you get herpes, you have it for life.

4. Gonorrhea.   Gonorrhea is one of the oldest recorded diseases. It was familiar to the Chinese over 5,000 years ago. In recent years, however, gonorrhea has been upstaged by HPV, chlamydia, herpes, and HIV/AIDS. But that doesn't mean that gonorrhea has become trivial or has disappeared. Up to 100,000 women per year in the United States become sterile due to gonorrhea.

Gonorrhea (from Greek words meaning "seed" and "flow") is a bacterial agent that lives on warm, moist surfaces. It is extremely infective, causing a high likelihood (up to 90%) of being spread with even one sexual contact.

Gonorrhea more often produces symptoms in boys than it does in girls. Males are more likely to experience urethritis with gonorrhea than with chlamydia. Generally, the urethritis is bad enough to warrant attention by a doctor.

In girls, the gonorrhea infection again usually involves the vulnerable cervix, and no symptoms are noticed. Vague stomach pain and vaginal discharge are two symptoms of gonorrhea, but they appear in only 20% of infected females.

The absence of symptoms allows the gonorrhea infection to be quietly passed along to a sexual partner or to become a severe problem for women by ascending into the fallopian tubes. Like chlamydia, gonorrhea causes pelvic inflammatory disease and the consequent risks of infertility and tubal pregnancy.

Treatment of gonorrhea. In the early stages of infection involving the urethra or cervix, gonorrhea can be effectively treated with penicillin. In recent years, however, an increasing number of gonorrhea germs have become resistant to penicillin. Currently, it's standard practice to treat gonorrhea with an intramuscular injection of a strong antibiotic and with an additional oral antibiotic.

Remember, most girls have no symptoms of gonorrhea infection. If pelvic inflammatory disease develops, treatment is much more difficult. And PID-caused scarring on the girl's fallopian tubes, just like the scarring caused by chlamydia, can be permanent.

Infertility is so devastating, it often disorients my patients to life itself. This is more than shock or even depression. It impacts on every aspect of their lives, including their marriage.... If you hope to become a mother or a father some day, don't play around.

—Dr. Joe S. McIlhaney, gynecologist and specialist in infertility [4]

5. Syphilis. Syphilis is another "old-time" STD. It is thought that syphilis originated during the time of the ancient Greeks and Romans; evidence of a virus associated with syphilis has been discovered in the skeletal remains of Native Americans. Syphilis was quite widespread earlier this century, and was responsible for about 20% of all placements of people in mental institutions because of brain damage from this infection.

By the mid-1950s, successful public health measures and the availability of antibiotics markedly reduced the level of syphilis infection in developed countries. But current statistics show that syphilis is making a comeback; it's currently at a 40-year high in North America.

The highest levels of syphilis infection occur in large urban areas. There's a definite relationship between syphilis, the drug culture, and the HIV/AIDS epidemic. This latest news is unfortunate because syphilis is a very dangerous STD.

The chief symptom of syphilis is the chancre sore. This painless sore, or ulcer, appears anywhere on the genitals between ten to ninety days after contact with the syphilis bacteria during sexual activity. Often it goes undetected because it is not in an obvious place. In any case the chancre heals up after about three to six weeks.

Usually, syphilis is unknowingly passed from one sexual partner to another, due to its high degree of contagiousness and minimal early symptoms.

Untreated, syphilis progresses through a series of stages over many years. In the later stages, destructive lesions may develop in many different tissues—including skin, bone, the liver, heart vessels, and the brain. These lesions can cause ailments like blindness, liver and heart diseases, various mental disorders, and death.

Treatment of syphilis. Syphilis is readily detectable by blood testing. Antibiotics are highly effective in the early stages of the disease, but much less so for the varied destructive lesions that occur in late syphilis.

6. HIV/AIDS. AIDS (acquired immunodeficiency syndrome) is the STD that you've probably heard the most about. The culprit of this disease is the human immunodeficiency virus which was first identified in 1981 and leads to AIDS. Since that time AIDS has become a worldwide epidemic.

In 1993 about 340,000 people in the United States had AIDS, according to estimates by the Centers for Disease Control and Prevention. As many as one million people in the United States are infected with HIV. About one out of four new HIV infections occurs in people 22 years old or younger. AIDS is now one of the three main causes of death in men and women between the ages of 25 and 44 in the United States. Medical experts agree that these statistics are likely to get even more dire by the turn of the century.

How do you catch the AIDS-causing HIV? First, you *can't* be infected with HIV through casual, non-sexual contact (like holding hands with someone who is HIV-infected or by touching a toilet seat).

HIV infection is spread through the exchange of body fluids between one person and another. The HIV-transmitting body fluids include: blood, semen, vaginal fluid, and a mother's milk. (As far as we know, HIV is probably not transmitted by sweat, tears, and urine.)

You can get HIV infection by:

- having vaginal intercourse with a person who is HIV-infected;

- having anal intercourse with an infected person;

- having oral sex (contact between one's mouth and the genitals of another) with an infected person;

- using an intravenous needle contaminated by HIV-infected blood;

- getting a blood transfusion of HIV-contaminated blood, or having contaminated blood enter an open wound on your body;

- being a baby in the womb of an HIV-infected mother or nursing from an infected mother.

Although there are not yet any known cases of HIV being transmitted through human saliva, saliva has been known to contain HIV. For that reason, the U. S. Department of Health and Human Services guidelines on AIDS prevention include the recommendation to "avoid open-mouthed, intimate kissing."

In North America, the majority of HIV infection occurs in homosexual men and intravenous drug users. But in many countries in the world (where homosexual and intravenous blood-to-blood contact is limited) the major mode of spreading HIV is through heterosexual contact. In North America, we are now seeing a dramatic upsurge in HIV spread through male-female sexual contact.

Of all the "sneaky" STDs, HIV infection is the most hidden. Very shortly after becoming infected with HIV, a person may experience a brief flu-like illness. This quickly disappears, and for approximately eight to twelve years, nothing may seem to be wrong. During this time, basically normal health appears preserved. But silently, the body's defense, or immune system, is being gradually and systematically destroyed by HIV.

HIV carries out this destruction by first concentrating itself on the body's lymphoid, or immunity tissues. As these vital tissues are gradually killed by the virus, the cells responsible for fighting infections and other illnesses steadily decline in number.

A person's health is endangered as infections that normally would be of minor importance take hold over the body's weakened defense system. At this point, the HIV infection has moved to its "endstage," or AIDS, which is 100% fatal.

Until full-blown AIDS develops, HIV infection produces no sores or other visible symptoms. Many HIV-infected people are completely unaware that they carry the virus. Only a blood test can determine for a fact whether or not a person carries the virus.

Treatment of HIV. Some medications are available for HIV infection that slow the apparent destruction of the immune system and the spread of the virus. No treatment, however, has been shown to prolong the life-span of an AIDS victim significantly. There is hope for an HIV vaccine one day, but none is currently on the horizon.

The HIV epidemic is relentlessly progressing. If you don't already know someone with AIDS, it won't be long before you will. HIV can be transmitted from one person to another during just one sexual encounter. This in itself is a powerful reason to save sex for marriage.

Other Points to Consider

We've discussed six of the most serious STDs in North America. There are more than 30 other sexually transmitted agents. At least one more STD—Hepatitis B—has rapidly become a major problem worldwide and a growing threat in North America. Hepatitis B can be classified as an STD because sexual transmission accounts for 30% of its spread. It is now the sixth leading cause of death worldwide. Vaccines are available to prevent you from being infected by this disease. Some of you may have been vaccinated against Hepatitis B as part of the U.S. public health effort currently being mounted to curb its spread.

Here are the other points I hope you will keep in mind as you work to safeguard your sexual health:

■ STDs often do not occur one at a time. That means that a person with one STD is at greater risk of being infected by another STD at the same time. Studies show a close link among gonorrhea, syphilis, and HIV infection. Young women with pelvic inflammatory disease often have two infectious organisms (gonorrhea and chlamydia) at work simultaneously. All these infections are spread through sexual contact. It is wise for any person who goes for treatment of one STD to also be tested for the others.

■ For women, the use of oral contraceptives (the pill) may actually *increase* the spread of infection and the likelihood of getting infected by several STDs. One reason for this is that because the pill reduces a woman's normal hormonal activity it may also reduce natural factors that protect against STDs—for example, it may cause changes in cervical mucus or the sensitive cervical transformation zone.

These physical changes may lead to an increased susceptibility to the disease-causing germs.

■ The presence of *any* type of genital infection, but particularly genital ulcers such as herpes or syphilis, *dramatically increases the risk of developing HIV/AIDS infection* if you are exposed to that virus. This increased risk is due to the fact that any break in the normal skin that lines the genitals can allow HIV to more easily invade the body.

■ You may wonder, "What if I or the person I marry has contracted a sexually transmitted disease? How can we avoid passing on an STD to one another?" The answer is that before you get married, you should see your physician for a premarital check-up. If you or your spouse-to-be has been sexually active before marriage, you owe it to each other to be sure you do not have an STD, or to be treated if a sexually transmitted disease is discovered. Even if you've never before been sexually active, the exam is still important to determine your overall health, as well as the health and normalcy of your sexual/reproductive system.

I'd like to offer some words of advice in closing. As a doctor, I would urge you to take good care of yourself—to do everything possible to keep yourself healthy and to maximize your chances, if you intend to marry, of bringing a healthy body to your marriage. If you do, you will not risk infecting your spouse and you will also protect your ability to bear a child together.

The sexual revolution has produced a dangerous, invisible epidemic. The sexual relationship between a loving couple in marriage can be compared to a beautiful meadow. Outside of marriage it may better be compared to a minefield.

Truly, the best way to avoid *all* risk of *all* these STDs is to abstain from all sex outside of marriage.

Chapter 6

What Are the Emotional and Spiritual Dangers of Uncommitted Sex?

A less often discussed consequence of uncommitted sexual activity has to do with a person's emotional and spiritual well-being. Even if the girl doesn't get pregnant and neither the girl or guy gets a sexually transmitted disease, sex outside the committed relationship of marriage can have hurtful emotional and spiritual consequences.

Human sex is not a purely physical phenomenon as it is with animals. For people, the emotional and spiritual dimension of sex is what makes it distinctively human.

So, if we want to understand human sexuality, we need to understand more of each of these dimensions. What are the emotional and spiritual consequences of sex without the love that can only be expressed in a permanent, committed relationship?

Some of the emotional and spiritual effects are short-term, but still hurtful. Some of them last a long time—even years, and can damage a person's marriage relationship. Many of these consequences are hard to imagine until you've experienced them. But all of the emotional and spiritual consequences of uncommitted sex are nonetheless very real.

Let's look at a dozen different issues that are involved in the emotional and spiritual realm.

1. *Worry About Pregnancy and AIDS.* Pregnancy and disease, as we've mentioned, are two very serious physical risks of premarital sexual involvement. Lots of sexually active people block these possibilities out of their minds altogether. Many others can't. The fear of getting pregnant or AIDS is a source of real emotional stress for plenty of young people.

Says Russell Henke, health education coordinator in Montgomery County Schools, Maryland: "I see kids going to the nurses in schools, crying a day after their first sexual experience and saying they want to be tested for AIDS. They have done it, and now they are terrified. For some of them, that's enough. They say, 'I don't want to have to go through that experience anymore.'"[1]

A high school girl told a nurse: "It's a relief to me to be a virgin. I see some of my friends buying home pregnancy tests, and they are so worried and so distracted every month, afraid that they might be pregnant."

2. Disappointment and Emptiness. Sex is a poor substitute for intimacy, as we saw in chapter 3. That's just one way premarital sex promises more than it can deliver. Here's the story of the disappointment one high school guy experienced:

I won't try to pretend that passionate physical exchange isn't enjoyable. But outside of marriage, the enjoyment is short-lived. When it's over, you're left disappointed. You start looking for another fix to appease your lust, like a drug addict craving another hit.[2]

Another guy speaks of a similar experience:

I began to notice that the more sex I had, the more I wanted. I had always heard that having sex was a way to get rid of sexual tension, but the opposite was true. Having sex increased my desire. It was like a drug. I couldn't stop myself, yet at the same time, I wasn't satisfied at all.[3]

For guys, the disappointment of sex may be physical. For girls, the disappointment is more likely to be emotional.

Girls, generally speaking, have different expectations about sex. They're not primarily after a physical thrill; they're not looking for something they can brag about in the locker room.

Girls are more likely than guys to think of sex as a way to "show you care." They're more likely to see sex as a sign of commitment in the relationship.

One study found that a majority of girls who had premarital sexual intercourse expected to marry their partners. Only a small minority of guys had that expectation.

If you're the kind of girl who expects a sexual interlude to be loving, you may very well feel cheated and used when the boy doesn't show a greater romantic interest in you after the sexual experience.

In fact, many guys, after having sex with a girl, don't even want to see her again—either because they feel guilty about using her or they don't want to get involved in any kind of continuing relationship. Says one 15-year-old girl: "I didn't expect the guy to marry me, but I never expected him to avoid me in school."

3. Regret. Girls especially need to know in advance the sharp regret that so many young women feel after having sex. Says one high school girl: "I get upset when I see my friends losing their virginity to some guy they've just met. Later, after the guy's dumped them, they come to me and say, 'I wish I hadn't done it.'"

Bob Bartlett, who teaches a freshman sexuality course at the Academy of the Holy Angels in Richfield, Minnesota, tells the following story that in many ways sums up a girl's all-too-common experience.

Sandy, a bright and popular girl, asked to see Mr. Bartlett during her lunch period. He could tell that it was serious. She explained to him that she had never had a boyfriend, so she was excited when a senior asked her out.

After they had dated for several weeks, this boy asked her to have sex with him. She was reluctant; he was persistent. She was afraid of appearing immature and of losing him, so she consented.

"Did it work? Mr. Bartlett asked gently. "Did you keep him?"

"Yeah, for a while," Sandy responded softly with her head down.

"What's a while?" Mr. Bartlett questioned.

Some tears began to fall. "Another week. We had sex again and then he dropped me. He said I wasn't good enough. That there was no spark.

"I know what you're going to say. I take your class. I know now that he didn't really didn't love me. I feel so stupid, so cheap."[4]

Sandy hoped, foolishly, that sex would help her keep the guy. Here is the story of another high school girl with a different kind of regret: she wishes she *could* lose the guy she's involved with, but she feels trapped by their sexual relationship. She also wishes somebody had told her the truth about sex.

Dear Ann Landers:

I am 16, a junior in high school, and like nearly all the other girls here, I have already lost my virginity. Although most people consider this subject very personal, I feel the need to share this part of my life with girls who are trying to decide whether to have sex for the first time.

In all the years I've been reading your column, I've never seen the honest-to-goodness truth about this, and I think it's time somebody spoke out.

Take my word for it, girls, sex does not live up to the glowing reports and hype you see in the movies. It's no big deal. In fact, it's pretty disappointing.

I truly regret that my first time was with a guy that I didn't care that much about. I am still going out with him, which is getting to be a problem. I'd like to end this relationship and date others, but after being so intimate, it's awfully tough.

Since that first night, he expects sex on every date, like we are married or something. When I don't feel like it, we end up in an argument. It's like I owe it to him. I don't think this guy is in love with me, at least he's never said so. I know deep down that I am not in love with him either, and this makes me feel sort of cheap.

I realize now that this is a very big step in a girl's life. After you've done it, things are never the same. It changes everything.

My advice is, don't be in such a rush. It's a headache and a worry. (Could I be pregnant?) Sex is not for entertainment. It should be a commitment. Be smart and save yourself for someone you wouldn't mind spending the rest of your life with.

Sign me

Sorry I Didn't And Wish I Could Take It Back[5]

Regret over uncommitted sexual relationships can last for years. We recently received a letter from a 33-year-old woman, now a psychiatrist, who is very much concerned about the sexual pressures and temptations facing young people today. After high school she spent a year abroad as an exchange student. She said she learned about sex the hard way and she wants to share those lessons with others:

> I was a virgin when I left, but I felt I had lived a protected life to that point. I got an IUD so I could make my own decisions if and when I wanted. I was dead-set against commitment. I was never going to marry or have children; I was going to have a career. During that year abroad I was very promiscuous.
>
> But the fact is, it cost me to be separated from myself. The longest-standing and deepest wound I gave myself was heartfelt; that sick, used feeling of having given a precious part of myself—my soul—to so many and for nothing, still aches. I never imagined I'd pay so dearly and for so long.

This woman says she is happily married now and has a good sexual relationship with her husband. But she still carries the emotional scar of those early sexual experiences. She wants young people to know that "sex without commitment is very risky for the heart."

Bunch of Thyme

Once I had a bunch of thyme;
I swore it never would decay.
There came a lofty sailor,
Who chanced to pass my way,
He stole my bunch of thyme away.

For thyme, it is a precious thing.
And thyme brings all things to my mind.
Thyme with all its flavors,
Along with all its joys,
Yes, thyme brings all things to my mind.

Come all ye maidens, young and fair.
All you that are bloomin' in your prime.
Always beware, and keep your garden fair.
Let no man steal away your thyme.

Old Irish Ballad

This song was written many years ago, but the message is no less true today. In this ballad, thyme, an herb, is the symbol of innocence or virginity. When a woman gives herself completely to a man, she crosses an invisible line which she, herself, may never have known existed before.

Regardless of the world's messages, the first time a woman comes to know a man completely, she realizes what it is like to have someone touch her very soul. Often it is only afterwards that a woman realizes how special was the gift she gave away—or allowed someone to steal.

—Alanna Payn Boudreau,
singer and songwriter.

---

4. Guilt. Guilt is a special form of regret. It is a strong warning that you have done something morally wrong. Guilt is a productive feeling when it reminds you of your values and reinforces positive behavior. When you don't listen to guilt's warning, however, it can take a very strong grip on you and control much of your life for years to come.

In his book *Love, Dating, and Sex* (which we recommend highly),[6] George Eager tells the story of a well-known speaker who was addressing a high school assembly. A student asked him, "What do you most regret about your high school days?"

The speaker answered, "The thing I most regret is the time I singlehandedly destroyed a girl."

Eager offers this advice to young men: "When the breakup comes, it's usually a lot tougher on the girls than it is on the guys. It's not something you want on your conscience—that you caused a girl to have deep emotional problems."

One 16-year-old boy says he stopped having sex with girls when he saw the pain he was causing them. "You see them crying and confused. They say they love you, but you don't love them." Another high school boy experienced pangs of guilt when he discovered he had a serious sexually transmitted disease and may have passed it on to some of the 13 girls he had had sex with.

Even in an age of sexual liberation, a lot of people who are having sex nevertheless feel guilty about it. Guilt is a voice of conscience telling us that we did something wrong.

Guilt may come from seeing the hurt you've caused other people. Guilt may come from knowing that your parents would not approve if they knew you were having sex. It may stem from your religion. Christianity, for example, teaches that sex is for marriage and that premarital sex is a serious sin. God and religion may not be in the forefront of your mind right now, but even if they're somewhere in the background, what you have been taught about God and sinful behavior is still a part of you.

Sometimes guilt gets a grip on a person and won't let go. Said one mother to her teenage daughter: "I had sex before marriage. Even though I knew it was wrong, I tried to make myself think it was right because we were engaged. That didn't help. The guilt still haunts me every time I have sex now...."

People who experience this kind of guilt should seek God's forgiveness and seek to forgive themselves. For most people this will bring peace. For others, however, feelings of unhealthy guilt may persist, and may require special counseling.

5. *Loss of Self-Respect and Self-Esteem.* Emotional hurts can also have a lot to do with how you feel about yourself. Sex without commitment can lower the self-respect and self-esteem of both the user and the used.

We were at a small college in New England recently for a conference with student leaders to discuss what they could do to create a better college environment. We made the case for promoting chastity as a way of establishing patterns of genuine respect between college men and women.

Afterwards, in one of the small groups, one young man said to us: "You do feel pretty crummy when you get drunk at a party and have sex with some girl, and then the next morning you can't remember who she was."

Here's what another college guy recalled about his high-school sexual experience:

I finally got a girl into bed—actually it was in a car—when I was 17. I thought it was the hottest thing there was, but then she started saying she loved me and getting clingy.

I figured out that there had probably been a dozen guys before me who thought they had "conquered" her, but who were really just objects of her need for security. That realization took all the wind out of my sails. I couldn't respect someone who gave in as easy as she did.

I was amazed to find that after four weeks of having sex as often as I wanted, I was tired of her. I didn't see any point in continuing the relationship. I finally dumped her, which made me feel even worse, because I could see that she was hurting. I felt pretty low.[7]

People aren't things. They are not meant to be used, then thrown away. People who exploit people in this way not only hurt others, they damage their own character and lose respect for themselves as well.

Lying in order to get sex is another way that sexual activity can corrupt character. The Medical Institute for Sexual Health reports: "Almost all studies show that many sexually active people will lie if they think it will help them have sex."[8]

Sometimes the lie is "I love you." Sometimes the lie is "You're the first one," or "I've only had sex with a few other people," or "I'm not seeing anybody else." Another lie could be "I've never had a sexually transmitted disease" or "I just tested negative for HIV." A person into a pattern of lying is going to have a difficult time maintaining any self-respect.

Many people also suffer a loss of self-esteem when they find out that they do have a sexually transmitted disease. For example, according to the Medical Institute for Sexual Health, more than 80% of people with herpes say they feel "less confident" and "less desirable sexually."

6. A Lack of Trust and Fear of Commitment. Guys or girls who feel used or betrayed after a sexual relationship breaks up may experience difficulty with future relationships. Some people may bounce from one short-lived encounter to the next after a breakup.

But other people, once burned, withdraw. They have trouble trusting. They don't want to be burned again.

Often, it's the girl this happens to. She begins to see guys as interested in one thing: sex. Says one girl: "Besides feeling cheap (after several sexual relationships), I began to wonder if there would ever be anyone who would love and accept me without demanding that I do something with my body to earn that love."[9]

Guys also have a difficult time trusting and committing to someone after a broken relationship that involved sex. Brian, a college senior, tells how that happened to him:

> I first had intercourse with my girlfriend when we were 15. I'd been going with her for almost a year, and I loved her very much. She was friendly, outgoing, charismatic. We'd done everything but have intercourse, and then one night she asked if we could go all the way.
>
> A few days later, we broke up. It was the most painful time of my life. I had opened myself up to her more than I had to anybody, even my parents.
>
> I was depressed, moody, and nervous. My friends dropped me because I was so bummed out. I felt like a failure. I dropped out of sports. My grades weren't terrific.

I didn't go out again until I got to college. I've had
mostly one-night stands in the last couple of years.
I'm afraid of falling in love.[10]

> You didn't get pregnant. You didn't get AIDS. So why
> do you feel so bad?
>
> —Leslee Unruh

7. Betrayal Turned to Rage. Sometimes the emotional reaction to being dropped by someone is even worse. Violent, explosive behavior—rage—is more and more often a result of a broken relationship. For example, in a small town not far from where we live, a 15-year-old girl recently stood trial for murder. She was charged in the shooting death of one of the most popular guys at her high school.

He was a senior and the star quarterback of the football team. The year before, when she was only in ninth-grade, she started going out with him. They had sex. Then she heard rumors that he was having sex with other girls, too. She became extremely jealous and confronted him. He laughed, and she became even more furious. A few days later she brought a gun to school and fatally shot him.

Our local paper recently carried another account of a similar tragedy. A 27-year-old man—call him Scott—was charged with killing another man his same age.

Scott had been living with his girlfriend Linda for a year-and-a-half. It was his first serious relationship. They had made plans to marry; they had even put a down payment on a wedding gown and reserved a date. Then, with no warning or explanation, Linda moved out of the apartment and took all of her things with her.

Scott said, "I was confused. I didn't know what to do, where to turn. I couldn't eat or sleep. I made excuses not to go to work because I couldn't hold my composure."

When Scott found that Linda was dating another guy, he lost it. He went into a jealous rage, confronted the new boyfriend, and stabbed him to death.

You might acknowledge the connection between the violence in these stories and sex, but also wonder, "Couldn't people feel really angry when somebody dumps them, even if sex has *not* been involved?"

Sure. But the sense of betrayal is usually much greater if sex has been part of the relationship. Sex can be very misleading. It can lead a person to think that the relationship is really serious, that both people really love each other. It can create a very strong emotional bond that hurts terribly when it's ruptured—especially if one person realized that the other person never had the same commitment. The resulting sense of betrayal may give rise to rage, and even violence.

8. Suicide. Sometimes the emotional turmoil caused by the rupture of a sexual relationship leads to deep depression. The depression, in turn, may lead some people to kill themselves. Teen suicide has tripled in the past 25 years.

In *Sex and the Teenager*, Kieran Sawyer writes: "The more the relationship seems like real love, the more the young person is likely to invest, and the deeper the pain and hurt if the relationship breaks up. The despair that follows a break-up is a leading cause of suicide."[11]

9. Ruined Relationships. Sex can have another kind of emotional consequence: It can ruin a good relationship. Sex becomes everything in the relationship. Other dimensions of the relationship stop developing. Pretty soon negative emotions enter the picture. Eventually, they poison the relationship, and what had once been a caring relationship comes to a crashing end.

One young woman's story illustrates this unhappy process:

With each date, my boyfriend's requests for sex became more convincing. After all, we did love each other. Within two months I gave in because I had justified the whole thing in my mind. Over the next six months sex became the center of our relationship. Like a cancer, it took over.

At the same time, some new things entered our relationship—things like anger, impatience, jealously, and selfishness. We just couldn't talk anymore. We grew very bored with each other. I desperately wanted a change.[12]

A young man who identified himself as a 22-year-old virgin wrote these words recently to an advice columnist: "I've seen too many of my friends break up after their relationships turned physical. The emotional wreckage is horrendous because they have already shared something so powerful. When you use sex too early, it will block the other means of communicating love and can stunt the balanced growth of a relationship."[13]

Kieran Sawyer summarizes succinctly: "A relationship that may have had the potential to grow into love can be sidetracked by sex."[14]

10. *Negative Effects on Sexual Intimacy in Marriage.*
When young people choose to have sex, they usually don't think ahead to the effects that their premarital sexual encounters might have on sexual intimacy with their future marriage partner. There are several ways that premarital sex can detract from, and even seriously damage, sexual intimacy in your marriage.

One problem is comparisons. If you have had sex with someone other than your marriage partner, there will be the tendency, sometimes beyond your control, to compare your spouse with previous sexual partners. Usually these are selected memories and often idealize previous relationships. This kind of sexual comparison can drive a real wedge between a man and a woman in a marriage.

Says one woman: "I have two friends who have to deal with the problem of comparing their husbands with the men of their past relationships. They fight the attitude of scorn for their husbands, who always seem to fall short of idealized memories of past performances."[15]

Sex on your honeymoon and in your marriage will be much more satisfying if it's free from any comparisons.

A second problem is sexual flashbacks. Sexual relations in marriage can be disrupted by involuntary memories of previous sexual experiences with other people. For example, Dr. Kevin Leman reports that many of the married women he counsels are troubled by these sexual flashbacks. In some cases the flashbacks have continued 10 to 15 years into the marriage. They are experienced as a distressing intrusion into marital sexual intimacy.

Men are vulnerable, too. One young husband writes:

I am married to one of the most wonderful women I've ever met. I would do anything for her. And I would do anything, ANYTHING, to forget the sexual experiences I had before I met my wife. When we start having intercourse, the pictures of the past and the other women go through my head, and it's killing any intimacy.

I'm to the point where I don't want to have sex because I can't stand those memories. The truth is, I've been married to this wonderful woman for eight years and I have never been "alone" in the bedroom with her.[16]

A third problem is the lack of trust that comes from knowing that your husband or wife had previous sexual partners. How can you be sure that person who has had sex with others before marriage will stop that behavior once married? At best, a person will have to teach him or herself a new standard of behavior after getting married.

11. Sexual Infidelity in Marriage.   In all too many cases, trust in marriage is in fact violated by sexual infidelity.

Cheating in marriage appears to be on the rise. In 1969, *Psychology Today* took a poll of its readers on sexual habits. Thirty-eight percent of the married respondents admitted to cheating on their marriage partners. In 1981 the magazine took the poll again. This time, nearly half of all married respondents (49% of men and 45% of women) admitted to cheating on their marriage partners.[17] Since that time sexual promiscuity among married people has continued to increase.

Why is there so much sexual infidelity in marriage? Think about it: If you don't learn to resist sexual temptation before marriage, what skill will you have to enable you to resist it after marriage? Premarital sex paves the way for extramarital sexual affairs.

Like any other virtue, chastity is a habit. It's developed through practice, through many acts of self-control. People who practice self-control before marriage are better prepared to practice it during marriage.

12. Lack of Personal Development. Premature sexual development can not only stunt the development of a relationship; it can also stunt your development as a person.

Just as some teenagers react to anxieties by turning to drugs and alcohol or developing poor eating habits, other teens turn to sex. Sex becomes a mode of escape for them. In using sex in this way, they aren't learning how to cope constructively with life's natural and normal pressures.

Teenagers who are absorbed in an intense sexual relationship are also turning inward and focusing on one thing (sex) at the very time in their lives when they should be reaching out—forming new friendships, joining clubs and teams, developing their interests and skills, taking on bigger social responsibilities.

All of these experiences are important nutrients for your development as a person. This period of your life is special because of the time and opportunities you have for developing your talents and interests. The growing you do during these years will affect you all your life. If you don't put these years to good use, you may never develop your full potential. You may never give yourself the chance to achieve the deepest and most personal dreams you have for yourself.

The risk appears to be greater for girls if they get sexually involved and close the door on other interests and relationships. Says New York psychiatrist Samuel Kaufman:

> A girl who enters into a serious relationship with a boy very early in life may find out later that her individuality was thwarted. She became part of him and failed to develop her own interests, her sense of independent identity.[18]

Remember: True Love Waits

We were at a conference recently with a woman named Dr. Carson Daly, who at the time was working for the United

States Department of Education. Previously she had been an English professor at a Catholic university.

She said that when she was a college professor many students (usually young women but sometimes guys) would come to see her, ostensibly about a paper they'd written for a course. Once into the conversation they would tell her, sometimes through tears, about problems they were having in a relationship. Sex was almost always involved. Dr. Daly comments:

> I don't think I ever met a student who was sorry he or she had postponed sexual activity, but I certainly met many who deeply regretted their sexual involvements. Time and time again, I have seen the long-term emotional and spiritual desolation that results from sexual promiscuity. No one prepares young people for these effects: the lowered self-esteem; the despairing sense of having been used; the self-contempt for being a user; the embarrassment of having a reputation that puts you outside the circle of people with true integrity; the unease about having to lie or at least having to conceal one's activities from family members and others; the extreme difficulty of breaking the vicious cycle of compulsive sexual behavior; and the self-hatred of seeking, after each break-up, someone else to seduce in order to revive one's fading self-image.

"No one tells students," she added, "that it sometimes takes years to recover from the effects of these sexual involvements—if one ever recovers."

Often, the scars from premarital sex sow deep-seated fears about intimacy or one's own lovableness. Sometimes these scars cause seemingly uncaused outbreaks of anger, anxiety, and depression, carrying over into other relationships, including marriage. Often, guilt about one's own sexual past ends up crippling these people when, as parents, it comes time to counsel their own children about sexual matters. "Because the parents can't bear to be considered hypocrites—or to consider themselves hypocrites—they don't give their children the sexual guidance they very much need," said Daly.

In Part 2—True Love Waits: The Dangers of Premarital Sex—we've presented three harmful consequences that can come from sexual involvement outside the truly committed love relationship that marriage alone provides. In summary, they are:

■ **pregnancy** and all the stress and hardships that result when pregnancy occurs before a young woman is married (including the psychological and physical risks for young women who abort their babies);

■ **sexually transmitted diseases;**

■ **destructive psychological consequences,** such as worry about pregnancy and disease, regret, guilt, loss of self-respect, shaken trust, rage and betrayal, suicide, destroyed relationships, damage to your marriage, and stunted personal development.

Keep these in mind when you face the temptation to enter into premarital sexual activity.

Part 3

"Safe Sex" and Other Popular Misconceptions

At an urban community center, a teacher asked a group of high school girls—who were either pregnant or unwed mothers—what they would like to discuss most. The physiology of childbirth? Care for their infant? Family planning?

The girls showed no interest.

Then the teacher asked, "Would you like to discuss how to say no to your boyfriend without losing his love?"

All hands shot up.

A recent article in the *New York Times* described a new sex education course being taught throughout California. The course not only teaches young people how to say no to sex but gives them practice doing it. Students are trained, through role-playing, to be assertive—to rehearse their refusal skills until they become second nature.

In one session, the instructor plays the role of the boyfriend, the would-be seducer. He tells Lori, a 14-year-old girl, that she is the only girl at her school who is not "hooking up." He says it's time for her to get with the action or "be dumped for someone who will."

Lori looks her "boyfriend" straight in the eye and simply says, "No."

The role-play continues. Her boyfriend increases the pressure. He says she must be stuck-up or scared. Then he whispers that he desires her so much, he'll do anything if she will have sex with him: beg, crawl, buy her expensive gifts.

Lori holds the line. She says firmly, "Stop pressuring me. I'm not into sex. I'm into education."[1]

Classes like these recognize that practical help is needed in order to stay away from premature sex and lead a chaste life. Unfortunately, much of the information about sex that young people receive—from school, the media, and even their parents—leads them away from chastity. This information is often based on the premise that teens do not have the desire or the skills to refrain from sex until marriage.

Consider the promotion of practicing "safe sex" by using condoms. At many schools condoms are distributed in the nurse's office. One school in California arranged for a gift pack of condoms and Planned Parenthood information to be distributed at the senior prom. "We were trying to spread a little responsible behavior," a senior class officer said.[2]

A college psychologist likewise argued that there is nothing wrong with teens expressing themselves sexually, as long as they use condoms:

> Let's say a couple has paired off, wants to be monogamous and uses condoms, I'd say that's a legitimate part of their sexual expression as a couple in the 90s.[3]

That message certainly doesn't support chastity. Neither does the way many school sex education programs talk about using condoms to "prevent" pregnancy and sexually transmitted diseases. In fact, condoms are not even close to being 100% effective in preventing either pregnancy or the transmission of an STD. And condoms provide no protection whatever against the emotional and spiritual hurts associated with premarital sex.

Says one 17-year-old girl about what she has been taught by adults:

Not all teenagers have sex. They're not all going to do it just because everyone else is. Parents and society in general kind of have a lack of faith in us.[4]

In this section, we'll look at some things you may have heard or been taught about sex. What is really acceptable and what is not for the person who desires to eventually find the fullness of sexual intimacy in marriage? Why is much of what's portrayed by popular culture about sex before marriage just not true? In addition, we'll look at ways for you to control your sexual feelings and at a question most people you age wonder about: "How far is too far?"

Chapter 7

Doesn't Using a Condom Make Sex Responsible?

With William J. Boudreau, M.D.

After we gave a talk to a group of teenagers on the reasons to save sex for marriage, one young person asked, "Why shouldn't we have sex if we have protection?"

Dr. Joe McIlhaney, in his pamphlet *Why Condoms Aren't Safe*, tells the story of "Jenny."

Jenny went to her doctor when she discovered a small growth on her external genital organs. A biopsy showed this to be a precancerous lesion. Left untreated, it would have required cancer surgery.

Told that the condition was likely a side-effect of her sexual activity, Jenny said to the doctor, "But how could this happen? I've been so careful. I've insisted that my partner use a condom *every time*!" (A condom is a flexible rubber or latex sheath that covers the penis during intercourse.)

Jenny's doctor explained that her growth—most likely caused by human papillomavirus—probably began when secretions from one of her boyfriends had spilled onto Jenny after sex, despite the fact that he had used a condom.

Jenny felt confused and betrayed. She had been "good enough" to practice "safe sex." How could such a bad thing happen to her?[1]

Jenny's unhappy experience is all too common. A great many young people have heard—and believed—the "safe sex" message. Condoms are promoted by the media and many public health and school programs as the way to pass unharmed through the minefield of premarital sex. Use a condom and you won't get pregnant. Use a condom and you won't get AIDS or other STDs.

Do the facts back up these claims? They don't, as Jenny's story shows. The medical facts show that condoms *reduce* the risk of pregnancy and AIDS but not to an acceptable level. *A very significant risk remains.* And condoms provide virtually no protection against some of the most common STDs like human papillomavirus and chlamydia.

Before we look at why that's true, we'd like to address a question you may be wondering about: If condoms don't make sex safe, how come so many people are promoting the "safe sex" message?

One reason is the pressure to "do something," particularly about the spread of HIV/AIDS. The safe sex/condom campaign seems like a "quick fix." A *Time* magazine report summarized the dilemma:

> In such a climate of fear, moral debate seemed like a luxury. Get them the information, give them the protection. We can talk about morality later. There is a fishbowl full of condoms in the nurse's office, help yourself.[2]

We've asked people who promote the condom "solution" to teen pregnancy and STDs: "Do you really believe that condoms make sex safe?"

One person answered: "No, there are still risks. But most teenagers are going to continue to have sex no matter what we adults say, and condoms are safer than using no protection at all. We're afraid that if we emphasize the risks of condoms, kids might not use them."

Is this logical reasoning? It is undeniably true that many young people will continue to have sex no matter what anybody tells them about the dangers—just as a lot of young people will continue to do drugs or drive while drinking despite the well-known dangers of those behaviors.

But is that any reason to withhold from everyone accurate information about the dangers of premarital sex, even when you're using a condom? Obviously not.

So let's look at the real risks that are still present even if sexually active singles use so-called "protection."

Condoms and Pregnancy

You can use a condom and still get pregnant. A variety of studies find that condoms have an annual failure rate in preventing pregnancy of 10% to 30%.

"Annual failure rate" means that, if you are using a condom to try to prevent pregnancy, in the course of just one year you have at least a 10% chance of getting pregnant. One study found a 36% pregnancy failure rate among teenagers, who tend to make more mistakes than older persons in using condoms.[3] For any condom user, the chance of eventually getting pregnant goes up steadily if the user continues to rely on a condom for contraception year after year.

The fact that a young woman can still get pregnant even when using a condom is pretty interesting when you consider that a woman is fertile—able to conceive—only a few days out of her entire menstrual cycle. How is it possible for pregnancy to happen at these rates for couples who have sex with a condom?

First of all, there's human error. Teenagers aren't the only ones who don't always use condoms correctly. Sexual excitement or the influence of alcohol often interferes with correct usage. There's a big difference between laboratory studies of condom effectiveness (using fluid-filled condoms to simulate real conditions) and real-life sexual encounters involving less-than-perfect human beings.

Besides "user failure," there is also "product failure." Condoms sometimes have holes. The sperm can get through a hole.

Pregnancy may also occur when a condom slips off or breaks during intercourse. A study by Dr. James Trussel, reported in *Family Planning Perspectives* found that condoms slipped off or broke 8% of the time during vaginal intercourse—regardless of the condom brand, the use of additional lubricant, or people's past experience in using condoms.

Interestingly, several studies have shown that high schools that have distributed condoms to their students have generally not been successful in reducing student pregnancies (even advocates of condom distribution have admitted this fact). In some cases the pregnancy rate has actually gone up.

For example, in May, 1992 *USA Today* ran a story about a "progressive" Colorado school that handed out condoms to its students. Less than two years later the unwed birth rate among its students "had soared to 31% above the national average." One explanation: Passing out condoms may have given students a false confidence that they could be sexually active and still be "safe" from pregnancy as long as they were having sex with condoms.

> *Young people need to know that condoms will not protect their ability to bear children.*
> —*Dr. Joe S. McIlhaney, Jr., gynecologist and specialist in infertility*

Condoms and STDs

Naturally, if a condom has holes in it, or slips off or breaks during intercourse, it won't protect you against STDs, just as it won't protect you against pregnancy.

But even when condoms do remain on and intact, they provide considerably less protection against sexually transmitted disease than they do against pregnancy. Why is that so?

The first reason is this: Whereas a girl can get pregnant only at ovulation time (two to three days each month), a sexually transmitted disease can be passed on from partner to partner *at any time of the month.* STDs don't depend on ovulation for transmission.

Secondly, STDs are very tiny organisms, minuscule in size compared to sperm. These super-small viruses can get through a hole in a condom much more easily than sperm can. For example, HIV (the AIDS-causing virus) is so small that two million of the disease-causing agents could crowd on the period at the end of this sentence.

A third reason is an extremely important fact that is not emphasized nearly enough by sex educators: a condom covers only a portion of the genital area that is contacted during intercourse. A female's pubic area and vulva are not covered by the condom. Neither are a male's pubic area and scrotum.

That's a problem, because the bacterial or viral germs that cause many serious STDs (such as human papillomavirus, chlamydia, herpes, and syphilis) do not infect just one place on your body. *They may infect anywhere in the male or female genital areas.*

So, even if the virus or bacteria don't get through the condom itself, you can still get a disease because the condom isn't covering enough of your genital region to prevent infection during sexual contact.

A fourth hazard: After intercourse, various potentially infectious sexual fluids are on both sides of the condom. As the condom is removed these potentially contaminated fluids can be transmitted between partners.

Medical studies show that for all these reasons, *condoms provide little or no protection against several of the STDs that are a danger to your health and your ability to bear children.*

For example, Dr. Sandra Samuels, director of the Rutgers University Student Health Center, discovered the following data while studying the cases of the students at Rutgers who came down with chlamydia:

- Women who used the diaphragm (a thin rubber device that covers the uterine cervix during intercourse) had an infection rate of 44%.

- Women whose partners used a condom during intercourse had an infection rate of 36%.

- Women who used no contraceptive had an infection rate of 44%.

These small differences in rates of infection were not statistically significant. The "barrier" contraceptives (the diaphragm and condom) had not in fact been effective barriers against disease.

Condoms and HIV/AIDS

The threat of becoming infected with the deadly AIDS virus is often used as the justification for encouraging people to practice "safe" or "condom-protected" sex.

But the reasoning in this area, too, is inaccurate. Medical research tells a different story: Condoms do not provide adequate protection against AIDS.

In one study, the University of Miami Medical School monitored couples where one partner was HIV-infected. Within 18 months, among those couples that continued to have intercourse using a condom, 17% (3 people out of 18) of the previously uninfected partners had contracted the AIDS virus.

None of those who abstained from intercourse became infected.

In 1993 the University of Texas analyzed the results of 11 different studies that had tracked the effectiveness of condoms to prevent transmission of the AIDS virus. The average condom failure rate in the 11 studies for preventing transmission of the AIDS virus was 31%.[4]

You might ask yourself: Would I fly on an airline whose planes fatally crashed 31% of the time?

Why do condoms sometimes fail to prevent transmission of the AIDS virus? A clue was offered by two Canadian researchers at the 1990 World Health Organization conference on AIDS. Drs. Richard Gordon and Natalie Bjorklund of the University of Manitoba presented a study with this unusual title: "If Semen Were Red: The Flow of Red Dye from the Tips of Condoms During Intercourse and Its Consequences for the AIDS Epidemic."

The study consisted of placing nontoxic red dye in the tips of condoms prior to their being used in sexual intercourse. The researchers were able to determine that during intercourse, drops of this red dye were pushed up to the rim (open end) of the condom. They concluded that "leakage over the rim may be a major source of condom failure."[5]

In view of the evidence of the major health dangers that remain despite condom use, it's not surprising that many leading health experts have stated stern warnings against depending on condoms for protection against AIDS and other STDs. Here's a sampling of their comments:

You just can't tell people it's all right to do whatever you want as long as you wear a condom. It (AIDS) is just too dangerous a disease to say that.[6]

—Dr. Harold Jaffee, chief of epidemiology, National Centers for Disease Control

Simply put, condoms fail. And condoms fail at a rate unacceptable for me as a physician to endorse them as a strategy to be promoted as meaningful AIDS protection.[7]

—Dr. Robert Renfield, chief of retro-viral research, Walter Reed Army Institute

Relying on condoms for "protection" can mean lifelong disease, suffering, and even death for you or for someone you love.[8]

—Dr. Andre Lafrance, Canadian physician and researcher

Saying that the use of condoms is "safe sex" is in fact playing Russian roulette. A lot of people will die in this dangerous game.[9]

—Dr. Teresa Crenshaw, member of the U.S. Presidential AIDS Commission and past president of the American Association of Sex Educators

A few years ago, Dr. Crenshaw was lecturing at a World Congress on AIDS in Heidelberg, Germany. Most of the medical professionals and counselors in the audience readily acknowledged that they recommended condoms to their clients and students as protection against AIDS. She describes what happened next:

I asked them this question: If they themselves had available the sexual partner of their dreams, and *knew* that that person carried the AIDS virus, would they have sex, depending on a condom for protection?

In a room of more than a thousand people, no one raised their hand. After a long delay, one timid hand surfaced from the back of the room.

I told them that it was irresponsible to give advice to others that they would not follow themselves.

The point is, putting a mere balloon between a healthy body and a deadly disease is not safe.[10]

An irony of the "safe sex" message is that by giving people a false sense of security about having condom-protected sex, the campaign encourages the high-risk behavior of premarital or extramarital sexual activity. In that regard the campaign contributes to *endangering* health and lives, not protecting them as is its intention.

When you think about condoms and protection against sexually transmitted diseases, keep these two facts clearly in mind:

1. Condoms provide little or no protection against widespread STDs like chlamydia, human papillomavirus, and herpes—because condoms often fail (lead, break, slip off) and because the condom doesn't cover all the potentially infected areas of the body.

2. Condoms provide some, but inadequate, protection against AIDS; the average failure rate is as high as 31%.

Condoms and the Emotional Dangers of Temporary Sexual Relationships

For all the reasons we've just discussed, condoms clearly don't make sex physically safe.

Condoms do nothing to make sex emotionally safe either.

The emotional and spiritual dimensions of sex are what make it distinctively human. Human beings have strong and complex emotions connected with sex. If we care about ourselves and others, we will be concerned about all the destructive emotional and spiritual effects that can come from temporary, uncommitted sexual relationships.

You'll recall our discussion of these emotional after-effects of sex in chapter 6. These consequences are different for different people, but they include:

■ broken hearts

■ lowered self-esteem

■ a sense of having being "used"

■ self-contempt for using another

■ the pain of the loss of reputation

■ compulsive sexual behavior

■ regret and self-recrimination

■ rage over rejection or betrayal

■ difficulty trusting in future relationships

■ spiritual guilt if one has a faith tradition that prohibits sex outside marriage.

Condoms provide zero protection against all these emotional consequences.

> "There is no condom for the heart."
> —A mother

Having Sex with a Condom: Responsible?

As a way to sum up, let's go back to the question that we were asked us at the end of our talk: "Why shouldn't we have sex if we have protection?"

In this chapter, we've tried to show that the "protection" provided by contraception is an illusion. The sad truth is that "safe sex" is a lie, a lie that can cause a person to suffer physically and emotionally, and, in the case of AIDS, even to die. That is why people like Jenny who are infected with a STD after using a condom are understandably angry when they find that they were not told the truth about *all* the risks of uncommitted sex.

Will knowing the real facts about having sex with a condom stop everybody from engaging in this risky activity? Obviously, no. But making a truly *responsible* decision about that sort of risk-taking would have to involve asking the following questions:

■ Does using a condom *reduce* the risks of premarital sex? (Yes.)

■ Does using a condom *eliminate* the risks? (No.)

■ What risks remain? (Pregnancy, AIDS and other STDs, infertility, emotional and spiritual hurt.)

■ Are these serious, even life-threatening risks? (Yes.)

■ Is it ever morally responsible to take serious risks with one's own or another's physical health, emotional happiness, spiritual welfare, and future life? (What would you say?)

Chapter 8

Isn't Sex Okay with the Person I'm Planning to Marry?

You may be in love with someone right now. You may even be thinking you want to marry this person. Or, you may be looking forward to meeting someone you would like to marry. When you do meet and fall in love with that person, it is natural for you to want to be as close to each other as you can. The physical attraction between the two of you is likely to be very strong.

Under these circumstances, isn't it all right to be sexually intimate? This is a genuine question young people have.

Much of society seems to say yes, it is okay, even a good idea, for a couple who are planning or considering marriage to have sexual relations and even live together before marriage.

In thinking about the sex and marriage question, it helps to step back and ask, what is the meaning of sexual intercourse?

To say "I love you" and really mean it is no easy task. For love is not only or even primarily a statement about current pleasure, enjoyment, and mutuality. True love, particularly married love, is a pledge for now and for the future, for the unanticipated as well as the foreseeable future. Christians believe that marriage vows are commitments, covenant promises to be there for one's beloved not only for richer, in healthy days, and in good times, but also to be there for the other in poverty or sickness or worse.

—United States Catholic Conference[3]

When two people have sexual intercourse, they're getting as physically close as two people can be. You cannot get any closer than that.

When you are married, this sexual union is part of a bigger union. It's part of a total public commitment you've made to each other. Your sexual intimacy expresses your complete giving of yourself to your husband or wife.

When you aren't married, sexual intercourse is qualitatively different. Not being publicly committed to each other fundamentally changes the meaning of the sexual union. Only in marriage can you completely give yourself to another. Even if you're engaged, you can always get disengaged; you haven't totally committed yourself to the other person. Your options are still open.

In fact, studies show that 50% of people who get married have been engaged at least once before. So just being engaged doesn't represent either security or commitment. You may feel 90% sure that you will marry this person, but until you're at the altar, you could split up.

Pat Driscoll, who writes and speaks on chastity, has a good way of explaining why sex and marriage go together, and sex and not being married don't. She says:

> Sexual intercourse is a *sign of marriage*. It is the physical symbol or sign of the union between one man and one woman in the permanent total commitment of marriage.
>
> A woman and a man are either married or not. Acting married before the fact is dishonest. Premarital sex is a lie. It says, "We are totally committed, but not really."[1]

Julia Duin, an award-winning reporter for the *Houston Chronicle* and author of the book *Purity Makes the Heart Grow Stronger*, puts it this way:

The greatest intimacy in life is sexual intercourse, and the greatest commitment is marriage. They should take place on the same day. Sex is an outward act that seals and signifies the inward commitment of marriage.[2]

The ultimate act of intimacy, in other words, is reserved for the most total of relationships. Marriage protects sexual intercourse from becoming trivialized. *You join your bodies when you join your lives.* Really join them.

From this viewpoint, sex before marriage is wrong because it separates sexual union from the total commitment of a man and a woman that can take place only in marriage.

Some Things to Think About

There are other things to consider about premarital sex. By having sex before you are married, you may actually increase the chances that your relationship will break up. Author Thomas Lorimer observes that premarital sex often "turns couples from lovers into fighters." Dr. Robert Blood, author of the book *Marriage*, reports this finding:

> Sexual intimacy produces more broken relationships than strengthened ones. [In a major study] more engagements were broken by couples who had intercourse than by those who did not ... and the more frequent the intercourse, the larger the proportion of rings returned.[4]

On the other hand, premarital sex may have an opposite effect: The sex experience can be powerful enough to lead a couple into a marriage that never should have happened.

When an engagement or any serious romantic relationship breaks off, it almost always hurts. But the hurt is much, much worse—and so often mixed with feelings of anger, betrayal, and guilt—if the couple has been sexually involved.

We have some good friends who shared with us the following story about their son Mike. At the beginning of Mike's sophomore year in college, he fell head over heels in love with a girl named Kelly. It was his first experience with "true love." "I'm crazy about Kelly," he told his parents on the phone.

Only a month after they started dating, they began talking about marriage. (That in itself wasn't wise; it's better to save verbal expressions of love and talk of marriage for much later in a relationship.) When Mike brought Kelly home to meet his parents, one of the first things they did was to sit down together on the living room floor and look at his parents' wedding album.

As time went on, however, Mike and Kelly gradually discovered that there were lots of things they disagreed about. Some of these disagreements were very strong; they viewed life much differently. By the end of their sophomore year, they came to the conclusion that they weren't compatible. They agreed to break up.

Our friends told us: "As Mike's parents, we have often thought how much harder that break-up would have been if he and Kelly had let their very strong feelings for each other lead them into sexual involvement. We are grateful to God that they didn't. So was Mike, especially when, just a year later, he had a new love—the girl he eventually married." Unencumbered by sexual entanglement, Mike and Kelly were both free to move on to new relationships without any guilt, without any scars.

Also—and you may be surprised to learn this—one of the problems in many marriages today is boredom with sex. In his book *Becoming a Friend and Lover*, psychologist Dick Purnell offers one explanation for this: The more you fool around with sex before marriage, the less exciting it is after the wedding.

"Before marriage," Purnell says, "your body reacts excitedly to the *forbidden* aspect of sex. When you marry and take the 'forbidden fruits' idea out of sex and heavy petting, you take out much of the excitement. You've conditioned your body to respond to the wrong kind of excitement in sex."

This is one reason why a lot of people end up cheating on their wives or husbands. An extramarital affair is "against-the-rules sex," and that, for them, is what makes it exciting. If you've gotten hooked on the forbidden aspect of sex before marriage, you're going to be more vulnerable to this kind of temptation after marriage.

In fact, however, sex with your marriage partner is "the best sex," as George Eager explains in his book for teens, *Understanding Your Sex Drive*. That's because married sex is with someone who loves you as much as you love him or her. And because marriage maximizes the likelihood of real love, security, and commitment, you can express your love for each other to the fullest. But you may reduce your ability to experience "the best sex" in marriage if you've conditioned yourself beforehand to respond primarily to the forbidden aspect of sex.

The possibility of pregnancy is another big reason to wait until marriage. A pregnancy can end a relationship, or it can force a marriage that shouldn't occur.

An acquaintance of ours—call him Jack—is an example of a case where the relationship ended because of a pregnancy. Jack and his girlfriend Lori lived together in Oregon for two years when they were in their mid-20s. During this time Lori became pregnant.

Neither of them believed in abortion. They had the baby, a little girl named Becky, and continued to live together for a short while. Then they broke up, and Lori moved to Colorado, taking Becky with her.

"She's got a new live-in partner," Jack explained to us. "She doesn't want me in her life anymore. She doesn't want me visiting my daughter.

"I grieve for my daughter. She's three-years-old now. I really long to see her. I'm going though a lot of emotional pain because this is my child, and I can't have a relationship with her."

The little girl, Becky, is a victim in this situation, too. She is being deprived of a father's love and all the other things that a girl needs from a father as she is growing up. As she gets older, she will likely experience an even deeper longing to know and see her real father.

Jack never imagined these consequences when he and his girlfriend were living together. They were just doing what everybody they knew was doing. But he and Lori's relationship created a new human life—a child for whom there was not a marriage and family in which to be loved and raised. That is a very big consequence.

Sex is so special that it needs a special home...and that home is marriage.

—*Pat Driscoll*

Wait Until Marriage

There's a lot of vague talk these days about "postponing sex" and "waiting until you're old enough to handle the responsibility of sex." We don't think phrases like that offer clear enough guidelines to young people who are trying to make the right decision about sex. Jack may have thought he was "old enough"; after all, he wasn't a teenager. He was old enough to pay rent at his apartment, buy a car, and help support his girlfriend. Before he got laid off from his job designing computer software, he was confident about his future career possibilities, too.

It's obviously not how old or "mature" you are that makes you ready for sex. No matter what your age, you can suffer the consequences—pregnancy, disease, and emotional hurt—that come from sex without commitment. What makes you ready for sex is the *relationship* you're in. And there's only one relationship that protects you against destructive consequences: marriage.

Says one 18-year-old unmarried mother:

I thought I did great because I waited two years to have sex with my boyfriend—until we were 17. Then we had sex, and a little while later we broke up. The next guy I went out with, I had sex on the third date and got pregnant.

To wait for sex, you need a vision of what you are waiting for. You need a vision of the kind of relationship in which sexual union is most fulfilling because it is part of the larger, ongoing union of two human beings.

In our society, in the wake of so much suffering sown by the sexual revolution, we are now rediscovering ancient wisdom: The relationship for sex should be one of *total, loving, and public commitment; namely, marriage.* It's within a committed marriage relationship that sex is most likely to be loving, the dangers of disease and hurt are minimized, and a family is available for raising a child if pregnancy results from the sexual union.

Marriage isn't perfect, of course, because people aren't perfect. Husbands and wives can abuse each other, and marriages can and do break up.

But marriage is a solemn, public, and legally binding commitment between two people—the most serious commitment that human societies have ever been able to devise. When you get married, you stand up in front of witnesses and say before them and God, "I promise to take this person for better or for worse...." You can't make a more solemn, serious, and binding commitment than that.

In *Sex and the Teenager*, Kieran Sawyer adds:

> The marriage vow is a *formal* commitment to accept all of the responsibilities that accompany a sexual union. To engage in sex without that formal commitment is to open yourself up to a world of problems, sorrows, and disappointments.[5]

These are among the reasons why wise people for centuries have said, "Wait until marriage."

Chapter 9

How Can You Marry Somebody When You Don't Know If You Are Sexually Compatible?

Recently, we sat in on a high school class where the students were debating questions of sexual morality. At one point, a girl turned toward us and asked, "What do *you* think about premarital sex?"

We shared our view about why it makes sense to save sex for marriage, the one relationship in which sexual intercourse expresses a complete commitment and giving of self.

After class, the girl who had asked the question came over to us and said, "I never heard anyone talk like that about sex before. Now I know what I think."

One young man from the class also stayed. He wanted to talk about something that was bothering him.

He was going with this girl, he said. We were pretty sure from his flushed appearance and the way he talked that they were into a sexual relationship. Then he said, "I don't think I could marry someone without knowing if we were sexually compatible."

"How will we know if we're sexually compatible?" is one of the most common questions young people ask, especially when considering marriage. Some people, both young adults and older, think they should sexually "test out" a person they might want to get serious about. The analogy they often use is that "you wouldn't buy a car without driving it first."

One obvious fallacy in this way of thinking is that people aren't cars. People aren't things to be used or tested out. That's not a respectful attitude to have toward people.

It's also not a realistic attitude. Eventually, cars deteriorate. The engine doesn't run as well as it once did. It may stop working altogether. But people aren't like that. People change and *improve* with love and learning. Married sex gets better as the partners learn over time what pleases the other.

> *You don't test-drive people.*
> *—Molly Kelly*

There's another big fallacy in the idea of having premarital sex with somebody to see if you're "sexually compatible." Recall the point made by the young man who visited with us after class. He said that he didn't think he could "marry someone without knowing if he and his girlfriend were sexually compatible."

Well, what exactly do you think he would learn about their "sexual compatibility" by having sex now?

Suppose his girlfriend is shy and inhibited or guilty about having premarital sex with him. Does that mean she wouldn't be sexually free and responsive within the security of marriage? Definitely, not. You can't project one pattern of response from the other.

Suppose they seem to click sexually right now. Does that mean the sex will be good once they're married? Not necessarily.

Says one young wife who recently got together with six of her college classmates from a few years back: "I was very surprised when most of these women said they didn't really enjoy having sex with their husbands. One even said she wished she didn't have to do it at all. The funny thing is, they all slept with their husbands before they were married."

Presumably, when these young women "tested out" sex before marriage, they and their husbands-to-be found they were sufficiently "sexually compatible" to go ahead and get married. But good sex before marriage doesn't guarantee good sex after. One reason is that a young woman may have felt pressured into sex by her boyfriend in order to keep him.

After marriage—if the couple does get married (remember, sex often leads to a break-up)—the woman may let all of her feelings of having been pressured into premarital sex come to the surface. She may resent the past and even begin to "hate sex." The point is that it's dangerous to play around with something that is designed to work right in only one relationship.

And, suppose, despite having had premarital sex, a couple has a good sex life in their marriage. That doesn't mean the marriage itself will be good. A successful marriage requires a lot more than sex.

You have to really know and be compatible with many facets of the person you're going to marry—their values, their feelings, their way of handling problems, their character. Premarital sex can keep you from developing that kind of knowledge, that kind of friendship. It can keep you from knowing whether or not you're compatible in these more important areas.

That's not to say that sex isn't important in marriage; it definitely is. When the sexual part of your marriage is good, it helps the whole relationship. And if there's a problem in your sexual relationship, and you don't address it, it's very likely to cause bad feelings in your marriage and perhaps even deeper resentments or alienation.

Nevertheless, when married couples are asked what's *most important* for making a successful marriage, they don't list sex first. They put other things—like shared values, caring, communication, commitment to the marriage, and a sense of humor—higher on the list. And almost always, if these things are present in a marriage, the sexual relationship will be good, too.

Beginning Your Sexual Relationship in Marriage

Some young people worry about being embarrassed on their wedding night if neither partner is sexually experienced.

In *Why Wait?* Josh McDowell points out that those who insist on "becoming familiar with each other's bodies" for the sake of a smooth wedding night are denying themselves the thrill of discovery on that night, "the first night in which they can do what only a husband and wife may do."

Part of the thrill of beginning a life together, as McDowell says, is learning about sex together, guiding and helping each other. That very intimate interaction is part of what forms a strong bond between a newly married couple.

So, it's important to know that when you get married, you don't need to be sexually experienced in order to be fulfilled in your sexual relationship.

You can grow together with your husband or wife and discover how to make each other happy in your sexual relationship, just as you learn and grow in other areas of your total relationship. This whole learning process is an important part of a loving sexual relationship in marriage. If there are problems, you and your spouse can talk about them with sensitivity, gentleness, and openness, and work them out.

To put it bluntly, everybody's plumbing works. What makes for a good married sex life is how much the man and woman love each other as persons. People who love each other try to please the other in every way, including sexually.

Chapter 10

What About Living Together?

It's common for young adults these days to move in with their sexual partner and live together. You probably know somebody who has done this.

When "living together" began to become a trend two decades ago, many people thought it was a sensible step, a kind of "trial marriage." If it worked out, then a couple could get married. If it didn't work out, they could split up—and avoid making the mistake of marrying someone they weren't compatible with.

Is living together really a good idea?

To answer that, we need to ask a number of other questions.

How does living together affect the meaning of sex?
You're engaging in the ultimate intimacy (sex) without having the ultimate commitment (marriage). You're acting married (joining your bodies) when you're really not (you haven't publicly stated your vows of commitment to one another).

What if you become pregnant? (Remember, it happens, even when you're using contraceptives.) What will you do if a new life begins?

What about sexually transmitted disease? You may not know exactly how many previous sexual partners your live-in mate has had, but there's a good chance you're not the first. Is your partner going to be honest about his or her sexual past, get a physical check-up to see what viruses he or she might be carrying, *and* get treatment for any STD that is found? (Remember, too, that 80% of the time people with STDs don't know right away that they're infected because they can't see or feel any symptoms.)

What will be the emotional consequences if you and your live-in break up, as approximately 80% of co-habiting couples do? [1] Will you feel betrayed if you went into the arrangement thinking (or at least hoping) it would lead to marriage, and it later became obvious that the other person never had those same expectations?

If you belong to a religious or faith tradition, what does it teach about sex outside of marriage? How would living together with a boyfriend or girlfriend affect your relationship with God? (This issue will be discussed in more detail in chapter 14.)

Is living together really a good way to prepare for marriage? If it were, you'd think that people who live together before marriage would be *less* likely to get divorced than people who don't live together.

However, much to some people's surprise, just the opposite is turning out to be true.

Seven different studies have all come to the same conclusions: Couples who lived together before their marriage are significantly *more* likely to divorce than couples who did not live together. For example:

- A U.S. survey of 13,000 adults found that those who lived together before marriage were one-third more likely to separate or divorce within 10 years.

- A Canadian national survey of over 5,000 women found that those who lived together with their boyfriends were 54% more likely to divorce within fifteen years of being married.

- A Swedish study of 4,000 women found that those who lived together with their boyfriends before marriage were 80% more likely to eventually divorce. [2]

So, if you really want to have a lasting marriage, one that avoids all the painful effects of divorce for you, your spouse, and your children, keep in mind that living together before the wedding doesn't decrease your chances of divorcing. On the contrary, it increases them.

Why Doesn't Living Together Work?

One reason that living together does not lead to a successful marriage is that sex can fool you into marrying the wrong person.

We spoke recently with Cathy Colligan; she and her husband John give talks on family life and are authors of a very helpful book, *The Healing Power of Love: Creating Peace in Marriage and Family Life*. Together, they also do counseling with engaged couples. Cathy said:

> We see many engaged couples who are living together. We find out by talking with them that they have little in common. They don't know each other very well. They haven't talked about their values and goals. But the sexual attraction and involvement are very strong.
>
> When we suggest that they not live or sleep together, that they try to become friends and get to know each other to find out if they're really compatible, they typically resist. They don't see how they can stop having sex now that they are involved.

As their counselors, we can see that this is a marriage likely to fail. And time after time, often in just a few years, it does.

Author and counselor Laura Schlessinger offers additional reasons about why living together doesn't work. One is that the live-in arrangement is demeaning to the woman. Schlessinger writes:

Moving in with a man when you don't know how he feels about your future together is simply an attempt to try to make him feel he'd like to share his life with you. That's demeaning and dumb. It's about you auditioning.[3]

As an example, Schlessinger tells the story of Diana. Diana and her boyfriend had been living together for five months. "Although she claimed that they constantly talked about marriage, actually *she* constantly talked about marriage. Her lover responded to her entreaties by saying he wanted to marry her, but he didn't know when because he didn't feel 'ready.'"

Diana's boyfriend was very content to let things stay as they were, while she kept nervously hoping to someday get the part of the bride.

Yolanda, a social-services professional in her 30s, called counselor Schlessinger to discuss a different problem that she was having with her live-in boyfriend of three years. He had just admitted to having a weekend fling with another woman. She was devastated. She had assumed they had a mutually faithful relationship. Schlessinger comments:

I pointed out to Yolanda that when you move in with a man without a commitment, he already knows one crucial thing: He doesn't have to do much to get you. Then he fools around, and you stay, and he learns something more: He doesn't have to do much to keep you either. And that has to be crushing to your self-respect.

Why, in Schlessinger's view, do couples who live together before marriage have a considerably higher divorce rate? She observes: "Having sex too soon, moving in without commitments or similar goals, are the behaviors of basically immature, let-me-feel-good-right-now people." Immature people, she says, are usually not the ones to persist with the effort and sacrifice required to develop and maintain a good marriage.

There's another reason for the higher divorce rate among couples who lived together: Women usually don't live with a man in order to check him out at close range. Rather, women move in because they want to be cared for and wanted.

They aren't wondering whether they want the man; they're too busy wondering whether he wants *them*. So they put up with, and try to work around, controlling, petty, immature, selfish, and hurtful behaviors from the man. They try to ignore the faults that may later wreck a marriage.

What's more, the very thing that attracts some people about living together—the freedom to leave—turns out to be a psychological burden once they're in the relationship. People living together have two questions constantly hanging over their heads:

1. Will the other person stay or leave?

2. Do *I* want to stay in the relationship or do I want to leave?

At any time, for any reason, either person can walk out the door; there is nothing binding to hold them.

Because there is no real commitment, no security in living-together relationships, couples may find themselves "walking on eggs"—trying to avoid touchy issues lest they trigger a conflict that could hurt or end their relationship. They hold back; they don't tell their deepest beliefs, concerns, or fears. They don't take a close look at their relationship to see whether they have enough going to make a marriage work. Although they may have thought they would "find out if we're compatible" when they moved in together, living together ends up making it harder, not easier, to find that out.

So, if you want to maximize your chances of a lasting, happy marriage, living together before marriage is not the way to go. *Be* together in a dozen different ways; talk together; learn together; grow together as friends. Those are much better ways to prepare for a successful marriage.

Chapter 11

Special Concerns

Our focus until now has been sexual intercourse. But sexual morality encompasses other important issues and behaviors as well. In this chapter, we'd like to address special concerns you may have questions about: masturbation, pornography, sexual harassment, date rape, and sexual abuse. We'd like to offer some guidelines for these areas that will help you apply a high standard of respect for self, others, and the gift of sex.

Masturbation

Many young people wonder, "What about masturbation? Is that right or wrong?"

One view that you may have heard some people express is that masturbation is perfectly normal behavior and a safe alternative to intercourse.

It's true that masturbation is "normal," in that many young people of both sexes engage in this behavior. But to classify a behavior as normal just because lots of people are doing it doesn't necessarily mean that it's normal in the sense of being healthy or good. For example, we wouldn't say that teenage intercourse is healthy and good just because lots of young people do it.

Figuring out whether masturbation is good or not takes us back to the question, "What is sex for?"

One answer is that sex is intended to be *relational*, an expression of love between two persons. From this viewpoint, masturbation is wrong because it reduces sex to solitary pleasure-seeking, sex with yourself.

Also, by its very nature sexual intercourse is meant to be not only *love-giving* but also *life-giving*. Masturbation thwarts that second purpose of sex as well.

Author Pat Driscoll points out the contrast between masturbation and proper sex between a husband and wife:

Masturbation is sex with oneself. Sexual intercourse is communion between a man and a woman. Sex activity with oneself is no union. There is no life or love-giving possible—just self-gratification.

Masturbation is partial, not holistic, sex. It offends the nature and purpose of genital sex activity. [1]

There are also good psychological reasons to avoid masturbation. Masturbation can easily become a habit that is hard to stop. If it does, your feelings of self-control and self-esteem will lessen.

It's also easy to use masturbation as an escape from emotions like anxiety or depression. If you fall into that trap, you're likely to end up feeling worse, because the problem that caused the bad feelings is still there. Better to face the problem in the first place.

Another important consideration: If you masturbate, you're going to have a hard time being satisfied with just hugs and kisses when you're with your boyfriend or girlfriend. If you're having sex with yourself, what will keep you from wanting the same level of sexual stimulation with someone else?

You'll feel better about yourself and better about sex if you can resist the temptation to masturbate. And you'll increase your capacity for sexual self-control in other situations as well.

Pornography

In *Love, Dating, and Sex*, George Eager reminds us of a well-known rule regarding computers: GIGO: garbage in, garbage out. As Eager points out, the same is true of your mind. If you put pornographic garbage into your mind, you'll get garbage out.

We would add a particular caution for guys, at whom most pornography is directed. If you look at magazines like *Playboy* and *Penthouse* or at pornographic videos, you'll soon be looking at females as *sex objects*, not people.

If you get involved with pornography, you'll also be arousing your sexual desires at the very time you need to be developing self-control. There are a lot of sad stories about people who got hooked on pornography—couldn't keep away from it—and subsequently got into wrong and even perverted sexual behavior.

A ninth-grade teacher told of a 14-year-old student who watched pornographic movies at home with his older brother and father. After several months of this, he sexually abused his cousin, a 3-year-old girl. A wife told of how her husband, a respected member of his community, got deeply involved in porn videos and ended up sexually abusing his 2-year-old daughter.

Pornography can also contribute to sexual problems in marriage. Some men become dissatisfied with their wives when they don't measure up to the air-brushed, breast-implanted models in the centerfolds. Some men even get to the point where they need to look at pornography to achieve sexual climax with their wives. Says one young husband:

> I used to be sexually involved and look at a lot of pornographic magazines, and it has messed up my marriage. I got so hooked on being turned on by those pictures that I still have to have them. When I go to bed with my wife and have sex with her, I can't even have an orgasm without a foldout next to her head on the pillow.[2]

The wife in this case was in counseling because her self-image was so damaged. She felt as if her husband was making love to the person in the picture rather than to her.

Remember: Your mind stores everything. Keeping your thoughts clean goes a long way in helping to keep your body clean. It's best to avoid pornography as you would the plague.

Sexual Harassment

The following incident was reported in our college paper:

> Jen, a freshman, was standing by the beer keg at a party when she was surrounded by a group of guys. They told her that in order to have a beer she must first repeat back to them a vulgar chant describing "how good" she is in bed.

Insulted, she told them what she thought of them and left the party. But, a couple of her friends ran after her and told her the guys "were just fooling around" and that if she left the party her future social life at the college would be "ruined."

There are several comments we'd offer about this story. The first is that you'll be happier—and will find more support for a chaste life-style—if you seek a more wholesome form of social life than the alcohol party scene. The fact that Jen's friends wanted her to go back to the party so that she wouldn't be cut out of college social life is a sad commentary on how desperate many young people are for social acceptance. It also points out how people often get the treatment they settle for.

The grossly disrespectful behavior of the college guys at this party also indicates a growing social problem: sexual harassment. Sexual harassment should not be confused with socially appropriate flirting. Sexual harassment is *unwelcome* sexual behavior.

A 1993 nationwide survey of public high school students found that four out of five students in grades eight through eleven had experienced one or another form of sexual harassment. Boys as well as girls are victims, but the effects of harassment on girls are much more severe.

The most common forms of harassment reported in this study were sexual comments, jokes and gestures; being touched, grabbed or pinched in a sexual way; and being intentionally brushed up against in a sexual way. Many students also reported being "flashed" or "mooned," being targets of rumors, and having their clothing pulled at or off.

The study also found that being harassed by peers was four times as common as being harassed by adults, but one in four female students said she had been sexually harassed at school by a teacher, coach, bus driver, teacher's aide, security guard, or counselor. For boys, the most often reported form of harassment was "being called gay."

The most common academic effects of harassment reported by the students were things like "not wanting to come to school" and "finding it hard to pay attention and participate in class." Girls were also likely to report "becoming more self-conscious and less sure of themselves."

Only one in seven students said they had reported sexual harassment to an adult. One reason for this is that some adults do not take these reports—especially those committed by adolescent guys—seriously. Rather, behavior like catcalling, pinching, bra-snapping, and even breast-twisting is simply explained as "boys being boys."[3]

We'd offer this counsel to both young men and young women:

1. Never engage in sexual harassment with words or actions. It's a violation of respect for another person. Here's a helpful way to keep in mind what is appropriate behavior: If it's not behavior you'd want to receive, have your sister or brother experience, or have your own child suffer if you were a parent, then it's inappropriate.

2. Do not tolerate sexual harassment in any form. Do not put up with it in order to seem like a good sport. Walk away from sexually inappropriate behavior and avoid people who act this way. You'll feel better about yourself and will command more respect from others. You will also be training yourself in two of the qualities helpful to maintaining chastity: a high level of self-respect and a reputation for demanding respect from others.

3. Talk to your parents about any harassment you've received at school and to a teacher or administrator at school whom you trust. If the problem persists, consider filing a formal complaint with the school administration or the school board. You have a right to be able to attend school without being subjected to any form of harassment.

Date Rape

Rape is the ultimate sexual harassment. The legal definition of rape is "a victim having sexual intercourse against her or his will, or without her or his consent."

According to the law, the victim does not have to be threatened with a dangerous weapon or injured for an incident to be considered rape. Threat of violence, or any kind of coercion, is sufficient to make the action unlawful.

According to FBI statistics, 29 states set new records for the total number of rapes in a one-year period in 1990. Rape is increasing at a rate four times greater than any other violent crime.

Lots of people imagine a rapist as somebody who jumps out from behind a bush or out of a dark alley and forces a woman to have sex with him. The fact is that an estimated 70% of rapes are committed by someone the victims knew; for example, their dates.

According to some studies, one in four college women say they have been the victim of an attempted date rape. In one in four of those cases the crime was completed; the woman was raped.

We had a speaker come to our campus recently to talk about the growing problem of date rape. She showed a film that was fictional but depicted a common scenario. It went like this:

> A guy strikes up a conversation with a girl on the way out of class. He's good-looking and smooth; they seem to click. He asks if she's going to the dance that night. She is. How about they meet there? Sure.
>
> They meet, dance, have a few beers. He asks her to come to his dorm room to talk. She agrees.
>
> When they get in the room, he closes the door. He sits down on the bed and gently pulls her to sit down next to him. They start kissing. He eases her down on the bed and lies down on top of her. More kissing. Then he makes the move to have sex.
>
> She protests. He says menacingly, "Don't play games with me, sweety." She looks frightened. Fade-out. The viewer is led to believe that the guy succeeds in forcing himself on the girl.

In cases like this who is responsible for the rape?

Answer: the guy is legally responsible for the crime of rape and also morally responsible for the rape. He has committed a profound invasion of another person's physical and spiritual integrity.

Does the young woman in this case have any responsibility? Certainly not the same kind of responsibility the guy bears.

Her responsibility is the sort you'd bear if you stood in the middle of a busy highway reading the newspaper. In other words, you'd be putting yourself at high risk.

We all have a responsibility to be prudent—to avoid, whenever possible, dangerous situations. The young woman in the movie scene described was foolish to go to the dorm room of a guy she had just met, foolish to be in the room with the door closed, foolish to get on the bed with him, etc., etc. She was an easy target. All said, however, the guy's responsibility is not lessened in any way. He still engaged in a criminal and immoral act.

Here are some words of advice for guys: Be aware that actions like those described in this story are illegal and immoral. Also, a few words of advice for girls:

1. Don't accept single dates with guys you don't already know well or know quite a bit about. Ask around. If possible, ask to meet his parents. Be in group situations first.

2. Don't ever accept a date with somebody who has the reputation of being sexually immoral.

3. Don't be alone with your date *or* boyfriend in a potentially dangerous area—a parked car in a remote area or an empty house, for example.

4. Don't allow a guy to put his hands where they don't belong. Forcefully tell him to stop.

5. If a guy does behave inappropriately in either action or word, demand that he take you home *immediately*. If he resists, repeat the demand and threaten to press charges if he does anything against your will. (It's also a crime to commit sexual assault; that is, a sexual encounter other than intercourse done against a person's will.)

6. If you are raped—on a date or in other situation—talk to someone you trust (your parents, ideally). Decide together on the best way to report the crime to the proper

authorities. A rapist would not get away with the crime and be able to rape again.

Sexual Abuse

Tragically, many young girls and boys have been sexually abused—often by a member of their own family. It's estimated that one of four girls and one of seven boys are sexually abused at least once by the time they are 18.

If this has happened to you, you should definitely seek professional counseling—to protect you against further abuse (if you are still in danger of that situation) and to help you heal the deep wounds that typically come from being a sexual victim.

If you can't go to anyone in your own family for guidance in finding help, you can talk to another adult you respect (for example, your priest, pastor or rabbi, school counselor, teacher or nurse). Parents Anonymous (1-800-421-0353) is an agency which specializes in dealing with child abuse. Call the toll free number 24 hours a day and a counselor will put you in touch with the nearest support group in your community.

We would encourage anyone who has to cope with this suffering to take the following suggestions to heart:

1. You're not alone; many other young people (who you may know) have also been through this.

2. It wasn't your fault—do *not* blame yourself.

3. From an emotional, moral, and spiritual viewpoint, you are still a virgin. A young person who is sexually abused is a *victim* of an unwanted sexual relationship, not a free and willing participant.

4. With help and time, people who have been sexually abused can and do put this hurt behind them and develop normal, healthy romantic relationships.

5. If you have religious faith, praying to God for emotional and spiritual healing and for the grace to forgive will help greatly in your healing process.

A woman in her early 40s recently wrote to an advice column to say that she had kept it to herself how her father's boss had molested her as a teenager. She was afraid to report it because she thought it would get her dad fired.

Finally she sought counseling. Now she deeply regrets that she didn't go for help long before. "It would have saved me years of depression," she wrote.

She added these words of advice:

> Please stress the importance of seeking help immediately after the molestation. Victims of sexual abuse should be made to understand that they are not guilty of any wrongdoing and what happened was not their fault. They did not ask to be treated that way, and they don't deserve to be robbed of their innocence.

Chapter 12

What Should I Know About Homosexuality?

A couple of years ago a speaker billed simply as "Joe" gave a powerful talk at our college campus. He was in his early 30s and he had AIDS. Once a sexually active homosexual, Joe said that a religious experience helped him to stop living the gay lifestyle. He made many important points about homosexuality that he had learned from his own experience. Several were valuable and can help you to understand more about homosexuality.

Joe pointed out what the medical and behavioral sciences acknowledge: *We don't fully understand what causes a person to be sexually attracted to someone of the same sex.* Genetic disposition, hormones, family upbringing, and sexual experiences are among the factors that may influence sexual orientation. How much influence any of these factors exert may vary from person to person.

In Joe's case, he believed that the lack of a loving relationship with his father when he was a child may have disposed him toward homosexuality. "When I was a kid, my father said I was stupid, ugly, untalented. I was desperate for emotional intimacy with a man."

When Joe was 11, he was sexually molested by a 20-year-old man. The sexual abuse continued into his teens. By age 16 he decided, "I must be a homosexual."

After many years and many gay sexual experiences, Joe settled into a long-term relationship with a man named Klaus. Though Klaus cared for Joe, Joe still felt unfulfilled. "I thought I had it all. Klaus was very handsome and good to me. This was a more intimate relationship. But I was still empty. Klaus couldn't meet my deeper needs."

Through a friend Joe came in contact with a Christian community that helped awaken in him a "hunger for God" and a desire to stop practicing homosexual sex. Joe said:

> They really loved me at that church. That's what churches should do. My whole life I wondered, "Could God love me? Did God love me?" God surrounded me with people who cared for me. I knew then how much God loved me.

Gradually, Joe understood that he was being called to chastity. Whatever the biological, psychological, or environmental influences a person faces, Joe said, "Your sexual behavior is still a choice. I believe I *am* responsible. It may not always feel like I have a choice, but I do."

Who Is Homosexual?

Many people—especially adolescents—experience a time of confusion about their sexual identity. Someone may feel attraction to a person of their own sex or have a person of their own sex demonstrate sexual feelings for them and wonder, "Am I homosexual?"

We have a friend whose college-aged daughter likes boys, dates, and hopes to meet a guy who shares her commitment to chastity. But since she doesn't have a boyfriend right now and she has a aunt who is a lesbian, she periodically wonders whether or not she could be homosexual. From everything we know, that's very unlikely.

Very few people are homosexual. You may have heard the statistic that "one out of ten people is gay or lesbian." That estimate turns out to be much too high and based on faulty research. Two recent studies have found a much lower figure.

In 1993 the Alan Gutmacher Institute published the results of its study of the sexual practices of 3,321 American men in their 20s and 30s. Only 2% of those surveyed reported any homosexual contacts in the past ten years. Only 1 in 100 (1%) described themselves as exclusively gay.[1]

The results of the Gutmacher survey were virtually the same as those of a 1992 study carried out in France. That study also found that only 1% of men reported being exclusively homosexual. The percentage of women who said they were exclusively lesbian was even smaller.

So, if you're uncertain about your sexual orientation, and the increased public discussion of homosexuality has caused you to wonder whether you could be homosexual, the odds—based on the recent research—are that you are not.

Respect for People

Like any other human being, a person who does have a homosexual orientation deserves to be treated with respect, love, and justice.

Homosexual sex (like pre-marital and extra-marital heterosexual sex) is wrong because it denies the life-giving and unitive nature of sexual love that can only be expressed in heterosexual marriage. A Christian attitude toward this or any other moral wrong is to "hate the sin (in this case, homosexual behavior) but love the sinner." In fact, everyone is a sinner.

In his talk Joe mentioned a father he knew who bought his son a one-way plane ticket to San Francisco after the son told him that he was gay. "From now on you're dead to us," the father said. That is certainly not an expression of Christian love. You may know people who tease, pick on, or are even violent to those they suspect to be homosexuals.

These behaviors are clearly wrong and one of the sad situations that often results from "homophobia." Homophobia involves an irrational fear of homosexuals (for example, the unfounded belief that you can catch AIDS by holding hands with someone who is gay) and often takes the form of hatred and hostility toward homosexual persons. Accurate information combined with the virtues of tolerance and respect can help to wipe out these wrongful attitudes.

Sometimes the term homophobia is used to equate moral judgments made against homosexual behavior with "prejudice" against homosexual people. This is an incorrect use of both the terms homophobia and prejudice. Labeling homosexual behavior wrong is a moral judgment, not a prejudice. While one may make moral judgments about a person's actions, it is wrong to hold prejudices against people.

Also, many people confuse *respect* with *approval*. They think that if you to respect people who are gay or lesbian, you also approve of their sexual lifestyle. This is a mistaken belief. Ethics requires us to respect people, not their actions. Respecting homosexuals means respecting their basic human dignity and their basic human rights.

However, people's rights may conflict, and some rights take precedence over others. For example, a child's right to a heterosexual parent as a role model takes precedence over a gay person's right to be an adoptive parent. No one has a "human right" to be a parent in the same way one would have a human right to life or free speech. Determining who can function as an adoptive parent is an example of a *civil* right that a society agrees to grant to its citizens.

Understanding the distinction between human rights and civil rights is very important. They help us think clearly about what are the legitimate claims of homosexuals and what is the legitimate interest of society in upholding a moral standard favoring sexuality.

Called to Chastity

A sexual act between two people of the same gender is naturally impossible. In homosexual sex there cannot be the complementarity of two sexually *different* persons in a union of body and spirit as there would in a committed heterosexual relationship. Sexual intercourse is also intended to be life-giving; there is no possibility for the procreation of life in homosexual intercourse.

People with a homosexual orientation—like unmarried heterosexuals—who wish to experience the fullness of life as God intended for them, are called to be chaste. Homosexual people as well as heterosexual people who never marry must control their desires and resist the temptation to have sex. Obviously this presents a more difficult challenge for homosexuals. Whereas single heterosexuals at least have a chance to

SEX, LOVE, AND YOU

be married some day, homosexuals do not. A homosexual's "call to chastity" is a life-long one.

Remember that living chastely, while a difficult challenge for some people, is not an impossible one. Consider the following stories of John and Vera, two people with homosexual orientations, who came to accept a chaste lifestyle.

John met Tom at a gathering of a Christian prayer group. They started dating and within six months had moved in together. John was happy in their gay "marriage." They had a beautiful apartment, great friends, and good jobs.

But as time went on, John was more and more bothered by the lingering feeling that he was still not living as God intended. "I particularly questioned why I felt so empty after Tom and I had been together physically. I had a distant sense that somehow God was expecting something else of my life."

Eventually John broke up with Tom and committed himself to a chaste lifestyle. He is now a brother in a religious order. He concludes:

Since that conversion, tremendous healing has come into my life, healing that I could never have imagined. My life is so different now that I hardly seem like the same person. I am growing into the man God always intended me to be.

Vera, too, was disillusioned after developing sexual relationship with a woman. When that woman became interested in a man, Vera became very depressed. She went to a therapist. He told her she should just accept the fact that she was a homosexual. "I wasn't comfortable with that," she says.

Most of the world says to homosexuals, "Accept your homosexuality; you have a right to express it." But for Joe, John, and Vera, homosexual sex and even committed relationships that had the appearance of marriage could not satisfy; they each felt a restlessness, a longing for something more.

Vera says:

When people say to me that they're happy in a homosexual relationship, I ask, "What do you mean by happiness?" The deepest peace you can have is when you're living the way God intended you to live.

Vera describes herself as living a celibate lifestyle even though she still has a homosexual orientation. She is a part of a Catholic organization that ministers to gay and lesbian people, helping to support them in leading a chaste life. As Vera adds:

A homosexual tendency is not who you are; it's a tendency in a person. There is a whole deeper reality to who you are. The more you grow internally, the more you can know yourself as you are known by God.

If you think you may have a homosexual orientation or are sure that you do (remember, most people do not), don't try to face your discovery alone. Talk to your parents. Talk to a priest or counselor, but be careful not to choose someone who tries to dissuade you from living a life of committed chastity. Pray to God. As the stories shared in this chapter attest, God can help you to commit or re-commit to chastity.

Is this all too hard? Hard, yes, especially in the beginning, but not impossible. With the support of family, friends, and the grace of God it is possible for anyone to live a chaste life. That is the life that God intends for all of us—the one that offers the greatest hope of peace, contentment, and happiness.

There are many groups that provide information and support to homosexuals who wish to lead a chaste life. Contact your local diocesan office—usually through the Family Life Ministry program—for resources and support groups that are consistent with and supportive of church teaching and a chaste lifestyle.

Chapter 13

How Far Is Too Far?

A teenage girl wrote to a counselor: "My boyfriend and I both think sexual relations belong in marriage. But we go a little further on each date. Now we're into heavy petting. Is this wrong?"

If you don't go all the way, how far should you go? A lot of adults may tell you not to have sexual intercourse, but they probably don't tell you much else.

One teenager says she got more specific and, she says, helpful advice from her grandmother: "Keep all of your clothes on all of the time."[1]

Another sound piece of advice is to stop at the lips (and keep the lips closed). That's because intimate touching (petting) and lovemaking arouse passion. Passion undermines self-control, and that's asking for trouble.

Petting is sexual foreplay, part of the process that naturally leads up to sexual intercourse. If you are into necking and petting, you have begun a process that may soon lead you to full sexual intercourse. If you don't want to end up taking that step, then don't put yourself in a situation where self-control will be hard to maintain.

As one high school counselor put it, "If you don't want to drive over a cliff, don't pull your car up to the edge and race the engine."

The intimate sharing of bodies belongs to the special intimacy and total sharing of marriage. Petting crosses the line between affection which is appropriate for unmarried, uncommitted persons and the complete giving of selves that belongs in a committed marriage relationship.

Beware of false confidence about how far you think you can go and still stay in control. Some people think they can get into hot-and-heavy necking as long as they don't get into touching private areas. That's still playing with fire.

Says Bill, a college senior: "The limit is going to move. You'll say, 'I can go this far, but no farther,' and then the next time you go a little bit farther."

In *Sex, Love, and Dating*, George Eager offers the following prudent guidelines that will keep you well clear of the danger zone. You are going too far, Eager writes, when:

- either a guy's or a girl's hands start roaming;

- either of you starts to remove clothing;

- you are doing something you would not want to be doing around someone you really respect;

- you are arousing genital feelings;

- you are arousing feelings that reduce your ability to make and carry out an intelligent decision.[2]

What if you have already been in a situation in which you lost control and went farther than you now think you should have? How can you back up and regain self-control?

It may not be easy, but there are ways to do it. Here are some very specific steps that author Thomas Lorimer recommends:

If you have already slipped part way or all the way down the slope, go back to the top.

For example, you will not be under as much pressure to succumb to temptation if you will respect all personal space. Cover up and be with people who are dressed modestly.

Refuse to tell or listen to dirty jokes, suggestive music, etc. Don't unbutton, unzip, or unsnap. Don't touch more than a hand.[3]

The advice, "Don't touch more than a hand," Lorimer reminds us, is a temporary restriction for people who have lost control and want to regain it. Normally, hugging and light kissing can be part of a premarital relationship where people have romantic affection for each other.

Once you do regain sexual self-control, Lorimer says, don't do things that will cause you to lose it again.

Don't start hugging or kissing if it will send you down the slippery slope.

When you do start hugging or kissing, don't let it be because you can't control yourself. Let it be the expression of self-control. You will be building toward a strong marriage.[4]

For all premarital couples, chastity educator Pat Driscoll offers this very clear moral guideline: "Stop at the beginning of genital arousal. Stop before lust sets in."

Molly Kelly echoes that: "There is a difference between affection and arousal." Don't cross that line.

Translated into a single, positive guideline: *Before marriage, limit your expression of physical affection to hugs and light kissing.*

Of course, some people will tell you that if all you do is hug and kiss, you're missing out on the big time. One 14-year-old girl said she had to part ways with her best friend because the friend was sexually active and pressuring her to be likewise. "You'd better get your butt moving," the friend said, "or you'll miss out on the best thing in life."

One of the sad things about our society is that so many people have fallen victim to this instant gratification mentality. They want it all, and they want it now. The irony is that by trying to have it all right away, you get far less. As someone said, "If you pick the blossoms of the orange tree, you will never know its fruit."

George Eager's book includes the following letter of a young man who wishes he'd waited before becoming sexually active. It goes like this:

Dear Abby:

A year ago, I started dating a girl two years younger than I. We fell head over heels in love. Our parents were friends and were overjoyed. They gave us complete freedom. When I would go to her house, her folks would go to bed early so we could be alone. At first we just cuddled on the couch and watched TV.

It was wonderful. We were together, alone, sometimes as often as six nights a week. We started necking a little, and then all the time. I started getting a little fresh, and she resisted, but she finally gave in from fear of losing me.

One thing led to another, and before we knew it, we had gone too far.

We started feeling guilty about what we were doing, but we consoled ourselves that we were "in love" and that as soon as she was out of school we'd be married—so what difference did it make? One night we had a terrible argument, and although it had nothing to do with sex, I know it would never have happened if we had behaved ourselves.

Anyway, she hit me, and I hit her back. I have never forgiven myself for that. She went running home and told her mother EVERYTHING that had happened between us. You can imagine what happened after that.

I was going to college at the time. I couldn't keep my mind on my studies. I just wanted to lie down and die. Finally, I knew I was flunking out, so I quit college and joined the Navy.

I saw her on the street just once before I left for basic training. She cried and told me she still felt the same about me and was sorry for what she had done, but it was too late then.

I'd give anything in the world if my girl had stuck by her guns and I hadn't been so persistent. Any girl who thinks she has to put out to keep a guy is crazy. I would have stayed with her if she'd only let me hold her hand. But I was selfish.

Sign me ...
A Sorry Sailor[5]

If you limit yourself to hugs and light kisses now—and save passion and sexual intimacy for a permanent love relationship—you won't be missing out. Instead, you'll have moments and memories of tenderness and romance that the fast crowd will never have. And you can be sure about one thing: *You may regret being sexually intimate too soon, but you'll never regret waiting.*

Part 4
Creating A Vision

A person stands out in today's world when he or she says no to sexual temptation. To say no to sex is a very public way of acknowledging your values, of letting people know what you believe in.

"Saying no" is not something you should save for the time you find yourself in the back seat of a car with a date. "Saying no" to premarital sex is a value that you need to communicate to others in your daily actions: in the way you dress, talk, and act.

Thinking of your "no" in this way is much like a coach developing a game plan; possible strategies are planned in advance for anything that might come up in the game. As you look ahead to situations that may threaten your decision to say no to sex before marriage, a good help is to keep calling to mind the vision you have of yourself: who you are and who you intend to be. Imagine how getting involved in premarital sex could ruin your vision.

But also imagine the good in waiting. If you say no to sex now, you can look forward someday to a very meaningful yes. You can look forward to saying to the person you commit yourself to: "I love you completely, and I give myself to you completely." That will be a very special moment.

We don't think we can express this better than two of the high school students who are part of a group of peers called the "Sex Respect" team. The first statement is by a girl:

One of the greatest gifts I will ever be able to give my husband is the total gift of myself. To me it would be a lie to give myself totally to someone before we've made public our permanent commitment to each other.

I believe sex is a deep communication, not just between two bodies but between the two complete individuals involved.

The second statement is by a boy:

I don't know about you guys, but I want a girl who's going to respect me and my values. I don't want a girl who will tease me and try to tempt away my self-control.

I'm saving myself for my wife, and I hope she waits, too. I think to have it with someone else would tend to tarnish the completeness and uniqueness of our totally belonging to each other.

I want to learn how to make love with the person I'll spend my life loving. [1]

These young people believe that chastity for a young person is true freedom—the freedom to grow up without the pressure of sex.

Unfortunately, popular reasoning is often value-neutral: "There is no right or wrong about sex—you have to decide what's right for you." Most of us wouldn't accept that kind of moral reasoning when it comes to drug abuse, stealing, rape, or murder. We know those things are *objectively* wrong because of the harm they do to the individual victim and to society as a whole.

In this book, we have been pointing out that there is also right and wrong when it comes to sex. One way we can figure out what's right and what's wrong is to ask, "What sexual behaviors enhance the well-being of the individual person and society?" and "What patterns of sexual behavior hurt the well-being of the individual and society?" You can look at your own life and the lives of those around you to find the answers to these questions.

In this section we will look at another way to answer these questions. We can find answers by looking at God's law and what God intends for us. Both reason and revelation lead to moral truth—with regard to sex as well as all other human behavior.

We will point out some of the other very real advantages of chastity as well as some practical strategies for living chastely. Finally, we'll give you a look at one of the best motives and rewards of leading a chaste life before marriage; namely, married sex itself and all that it entails.

It's true, of course, that the decision of how you will act is your own. Everyone is created with a free will; it's up to you to exercise your freedom responsibly.

We hope that in forming your conscience and making decisions about sexual matters—creating a vision for yourself—you'll make the decision that truly respects you and the other person, and that uses the beautiful gift of sex in the way that will bring the greatest possible happiness to your life.

Chapter 14

How Does God Fit Into My Decision About Sex?

Up until now, we've looked at sex from a physical, emotional, and moral perspective. But human beings also have a spiritual and religious side.

For most people, a spiritual or religious dimension translates to a belief in God. A recent Gallup Poll, for example, found that 94% of American teenagers say they have faith in a personal God. Most also say they frequently pray. So it makes sense to bring God and religion into a discussion of sexual decisions.

If you believe there is a God, you may want to consider a certain logic related to your belief. It goes like this:

If God created you, then God created your body. And if God created your body, God created your sexuality too. Sex is one of God's best gifts to you.

How does God intend for you to use that gift of sexuality?

Does God mean for sex to be used outside of marriage? Does God mean for sex to be part of the relationships between unmarried teenagers?

How can you know what God has in mind?

First, you can ask your parents. You can also ask your priest, minister, rabbi, or other teacher who has studied religious wisdom and teachings about sex.

You can also check what is written in the Bible.

Now, you may sometimes hear people say, "The Bible doesn't really say anything about sex," or "Jesus didn't preach about sex." Not true. If the Bible is part of your faith tradition, you can read it to find out what God does and does not want people to do with the beautiful gift of sex.

For example, the Bible is very clear about the sinfulness of adultery (having sex with someone other than your husband or your wife when you're married). "You shall not commit adultery" is one of the Ten Commandments listed in the book of Exodus (20:14).

In the Sermon on the Mount, Jesus expands on this prohibition against adultery. Jesus teaches that just as you can be judged a murderer by hating somebody in your heart, you can also sin against chastity or purity by lusting after somebody in your heart: "You have heard that it was said, 'You shall not commit adultery.' But I say to you that everyone who looks at a woman with lust has already committed adultery with her in his heart" (Mt 5:27-28).

What about premarital sex? The teaching of Jesus on fornication—as unmarried sex is referred to in the Bible—is found in chapter 7 of the gospel of Mark. Jesus explains to his disciples:

> Do you not see that whatever goes into a person from outside cannot defile, since it enters, not the heart but the stomach, and goes out into the sewer?
>
> It is what comes out of a person that defiles. For it is from within, from the human heart, that evil intentions come: **fornication** [sex between unmarried people], **theft, murder, adultery, avarice, wickedness, deceit, licentiousness, envy, slander, pride, folly.** All these evil things come from within, and they defile a person (Mark 7:18-23).

Jesus' teaching here is quite clear: Like adultery, unmarried sex is a serious sin.

That teaching wouldn't have come as a surprise to Jesus' first disciples who had all been raised in the Jewish tradition. In the book of Genesis, the first book of the Torah of Jewish law, God's plan for sex and marriage is laid out. Jesus often reminded his listeners of this plan as set forth by God since the beginning of the world:

> Have you not read that the one who made them at the beginning "made them male and female," and said, "For this reason a man shall leave his father and mother and

be joined to his wife, and the two shall become one flesh?" (Mt 19:4-6).

Notice the sequence of events in God's plan: First a man leaves home; next he takes a wife; *then* the two become "one flesh." The sequence is definitely *not*: First you leave home; then you fool around with a series of sexual partners; then, maybe, you choose one person to marry and settle down.

Saint Paul is known by Christians as the "Apostle to the Gentiles." Gentiles are non-Jewish people. Paul travelled around the Roman Empire of the first century Mediterranean world seeking converts to Christianity among the Gentile people. In many ways Christianity was a tough life-style for Paul to sell to these Gentiles who had become tolerant of and participants in loose sexual living.

Matthew Rzeczkowski, a Catholic priest and Bible scholar, summarized the letters of Paul dealing with sex in an article titled "Why Chastity?"[1] Rzeczkowski highlights four main points of Paul's teaching that were applicable to the first Christians and still apply to people living today.

First, God wants us to be holy. To be holy is to be like God. And we can seek holiness only when our hearts, minds, and actions are pure. Paul writes:

> For this is the will of God, your sanctification: that you abstain from fornication, that each one of you know how to control your own body in holiness and honor (1 Thes 4:3).

Second, Paul points out that sexual sin is a very personal kind of sin because it involves the abuse of our own bodies:

> Every sin that a person commits is outside the body; but the fornicator sins against the body itself (1 Cor 6:18).

Third, Paul reminds us that our bodies are not just our own: The body is a holy place—a place where, amazingly, God actually dwells. And, our bodies—in fact our very lives—have been restored from the effects of sin by Jesus' death on the cross. Therefore, our bodies are of great value in God's eyes:

Do you not know that your body is a temple of the Holy Spirit within you, which you have from God, and that you are not your own? For you were bought with a price; therefore glorify God in your body (1 Cor 6:19-20).

Fourth, Paul echoes Jesus' teaching that sexual sin is serious sin. Like other serious sin, it separates us from God until we are reconciled through our forgiveness and God's mercy. (Remember, that no matter how great our sin, the loving God is always waiting to forgive us.) In the letter to the Ephesians, Paul writes:

> But fornication and impurity of any kind, or greed, must not even be mentioned among you.... Be sure of this, that no fornicator or impure person, or one who is greedy (that is, an idolater), has any inheritance in the kingdom of Christ and of God. Let no one deceive you with empty words, for because of these things the wrath of God comes on those who are disobedient. Therefore do not be associated with them (Eph 5:3-7).

"Live as children of light," Paul implores later in the same letter (Eph 5:8). In short, Paul is saying, if you are children of God, act like it. Let God's Spirit show forth in every area of your life, including your sexual behavior. *Chastity should be a natural manifestation of God's life in you.*

Other Religious Teachings

You might be wondering if this is just the Christian way of thinking about sex. You may not be aware—a lot of people are not—that there is considerable agreement among different world religions about the issue of premarital sex. The fact is that *all* major religions regard premarital sex as wrong.

Consider these three statements, each drawn from a different religious tradition:

> Rabbinic teaching for at least 2,500 years has consistently opposed premarital sex. Judaism removes sexual intercourse from any context of selfishness or primitive lust, and enshrines it as a sanctified element in the most intimate and most meaningful relationship between two human beings. Within the sacred marriage bond, sexual relations are not only permissible; they are in fact the fulfillment of divine commandment.
>
> —Rabbi Isaac Frank[2]

The promise of two people to belong always to each other makes it possible for lovemaking to mean total giving and total receiving. It is the totality of married life that makes sexual intercourse meaningful. This is why the church refers to sexual intercourse as "the marital act."

—Father Richard C. McCormick,
Catholic priest[3]

Islam views sexual love as a gift from God. It is a sign of God's love and mercy and is given to human beings for their good and well-being. Islam limits sexual activity to men and women within the bond of marriage. It is permitted only to those couples who have joined themselves in a lawful marriage.

—Muzammil H. Siddiqi,
Islamic teacher[4]

Dick Purnell observes that God places sex within marriage entirely for our own benefit. When you share your body with someone, you're giving part of yourself. If your partner walks out of your life, something of you goes with him or her. You'll never get it back. Keeping sex within married love is your best protection against that.

So God isn't trying to rain on your parade. God isn't trying to spoil your fun by setting up a lot of strict rules about sex. Remember, God created sex. God knows that within marriage, sex is a source of many blessings, and outside marriage it is a source of many sufferings. Like a caring parent, God gives you rules lovingly, as a way to protect you against harm.

Sexual intimacy between a man and a woman is God's wedding gift to newlyweds. God's gift is not meant to be opened early.

—A young mother

Keeping the Faith

Finally, if you believe in a personal God, we would also encourage you to pray.

Why is it important to pray? Some of the best answers we've ever heard to that question come from a British Catholic priest by the name of Father Hugh Thwaites.

Father Thwaites was participating in an international conference on a perplexing question: Why do so many young people, even those raised in seriously committed religious families, stop practicing their faith—in some cases, even stop believing in God—after they leave home?

Father Thwaites said that, in his experience, it is usually due to one or a combination of the following reasons.

Sin. "When young people fall away from religious observance," Thwaites says, "it is most often because there has been a moral falling away. It is sin rather than syllogisms that turns people atheists."

Spiritual health, he points out, "comes from having right relations with God. To break the moral law is to offend the Law-giver. Moral disorder and spiritual disorder are linked together, as cause and effect." In other words, if you're doing things you shouldn't—having sex, getting drunk, doing drugs, lying, cheating, stealing—these sins, unrepented, will put a distance between you and God.

Lack of a personal relationship with God. The second reason for falling away from the faith, Thwaites says, is that the young person "never personally grasped its meaning." Religion was taught as a lot of externals, not as a means of cultivating an inner relationship with the living God. "If young people grow up without growing in intimacy with Christ, what wonder that their religion would come to seem cold and empty?"

Failure to pray. Thwaites recalls the story of a young man who was going through a crisis of faith in which he questioned everything he had ever been taught as a Catholic. The young man felt compelled to examine all the articles of the

Catholic religion one-by-one to test whether he could accept them or not.

Father Thwaites pointed out to this young man that intellectual examination of one's faith is important. But, simultaneously, he must increase his time spent in prayer. "If young people going through a spiritual crisis in adolescence give up on prayer," he observes, "they will come to reject their religion. Divine truths must be approached prayerfully, humbly."

(The young man in this story did increase both his time in study and his time in prayer, and three months later wrote Father Thwaites to say that he had come out on the other side of his crisis, with his faith stronger.)

Prayer as a Help Against Temptation

Nobody needs to tell you how many temptations and pressures young people face in today's world. And once you leave home and are on your own, those temptations and pressures will increase.

If you go to college, for example, you will immediately be faced with the decision of whether to go to parties where the expectations of many, if not most, of the people is to get drunk and have sex.

In the college community we belong to—no different from countless other college environments these days—we, sadly, see many students caught up in an oppressive and degrading pattern of alcohol, drug, and sexual abuse that robs sex of any meaning and leaves them with very little of their self-worth and dignity.

A senior who works as a residence hall assistant said, "We have quite a few girls in our dorm who have been pregnant and had an abortion. Some have had more than one abortion. A few of these girls have formed a support group to grieve their abortions—the day they had it and the day their baby would have been born."

Our heart breaks for these young people. We feel sure that many of them would have chosen not to get involved in such a self-destructive pattern of sexual behavior if they had had a vision of the meaning and beauty of sex within a committed love relationship and if they had called on God to give them the spiritual strength to walk a different path.

Prayer can help you to strengthen your relationship with God and, in turn, help you to resist temptations. According to Father Thwaites:

Not praying will not, of itself, kill the spiritual life. Only serious sin does that. But the absence of any prayer life will so weaken the spiritual life, that it will be unable to meet the onslaughts of a pagan world. People succumb to temptation through sheer lack of spiritual vitality. What food and drink is to the body, prayer is to the soul.

So, we encourage you to pray. Pray for God's guidance about what situations to enter into and what ones to stay clear of, what guys and girls to hang around with, whom to date, and how to act on a date.

Jesus once said: "Ask, and it will be given you; search, and you will find; knock, and the door will be opened for you (Mt 7:7). A slight adaptation might remind us to *keep asking, keep searching, keep knocking*. Part of the of the challenge of prayer is to persevere.

Also, know that the answer to your prayer won't always come in the form you expect. If you take a moment to look back at your life, you can probably list quite a few examples of things which you asked for and did not receive. If you look deeply enough, you may see how what God did give you instead was actually better for you. Then again, sometimes God's answer to your request is "Wait." This answer is in itself good; it helps to build a greater sense of trust between you and God.

God's action and answer to your prayer may take many forms. It may come from a person who comes ever so briefly into your life—even just a "chance" comment someone makes to you. It could take the form of something you happen to read. It could take the form of an obstacle God puts in your path that keeps you from doing something that would not be good for you or someone else.

It takes time and attention to recognize the hand of God in the events of your life. Be patient. Faith and trust is something that God usually reveals a little at a time. You can learn to develop this kind of prayer-relationship with God too. Talk to people who pray regularly. Ask them how they do it. Then set aside a time each day—even if it's only five minutes at first— to talk and listen to God. Then watch for the fruits in your life to grow.

You can count on certain fruits to be evident right away. Praying with trust in God's love for you will bring you into a closer relationship with God. It will bring you greater peace and security. And it will increase your self-control and help you to avoid temptations in the vitally important area of your sexuality.

We highly recommend a booklet called *Living Faith* ($5.95 for a full year subscription) to help you get started in personal prayer. *Living Faith* provides meditations based on the scripture readings taken from the Mass of the day. God speaks in a special way through the Bible and the shared communion of believers at Mass. These daily meditations take under 15 minutes. We think that you'll find that the more you pray this way, the more you will experience God speaking to you.

Living Faith
10300 Watson Road
St. Louis, MO 63127

Chapter 15

What Is Chastity?

Chastity is sexual self-control. It means placing sexual intercourse within one relationship and one relationship only: marriage.

Although we've used the word "abstinence" in this book and have encouraged you to abstain from premarital sex, we actually prefer the term chastity when talking about sexual morality.

"Abstinence" makes it sound as if you're missing out on something. By contrast, chastity is a *positive* moral choice and life style. Down through time, chastity has been an admired moral virtue. Author Pat Driscoll defines chastity as "sexual goodness"—living out the truth, beauty, and goodness of human sexuality. In one of her pamphlets, "God's Plan for Sex," Driscoll boldly states "Sex is great!" and then lists some reasons why it is:

■ God created sex, and it's wonderful.

■ God gave us operating instructions for sex (in the Bible).

■ Only the *abuse* of sex (through fornication, adultery, masturbation, etc.) is wrong.

■ Following God's law brings joy.

■ Disobeying God's law brings unhappiness and problems for ourselves and society.

■ God has given us many ways to express our sexuality—genitally (in marriage) and non-genitally (outside of marriage).[1]

Driscoll's final point is an important one: Chastity applies to *everybody*, unmarried people and married people. How?

For *unmarried* people (both those planning to marry and those who intend to remain single), chastity means staying pure in thought and deed, refraining from sexual intercourse and other forms of deliberate genital arousal, and expressing one's sexuality in non-genital ways.

For *married* people, chastity means having sex only with your marriage partner. This form of promised faithfulness between husbands and wives—giving themselves sexually only to each other, never to anyone else—is also known as fidelity.

Celibacy is a special form of chastity. People with a religious vocation—for example, priests, brothers, or nuns—take a vow of celibacy. As part of their commitment to God and service to God's people, they promise to lead a life that excludes all forms of genital sexual intimacy.

> *The more you have sex outside of marriage, the more it becomes just something to do.*
> —Molly Kelly

The Advantages of Chastity

Molly Kelly, a mother of eight, travels throughout the United States and Canada speaking about chastity to more than 50,000 teens and college students every year. Her audiences genuinely love her; she has a great sense of humor and a knack for using the right phrase. Molly Kelly calls chastity "saved sex." It's saving sex for the person you want to spend your life with.

When we heard her speak to a standing room audience of teens and parents, she said:

> Chastity is good news. You do not have to spend valuable time worrying about pregnancy or sexually transmitted diseases. You do not have to spend one penny on any outside product. You do not have to terminate your youth prematurely. Chastity is 100% effective, 100% healthy, and a 100% economical choice. It works!

She then challenged her listeners to think about the reasons for saving sex:

How do we want our air? Pure. How do we want our water? Pure. How do we want sex on our wedding night? Pure. There is no greater gift a man and a woman can give each other on their wedding night than the gift of their virginity. And it's a gift you can give only once.

But what if you haven't saved sex? What if you've already given it away? "Start saving it," Molly Kelly says. She adds:

Some gifts come with tags that say, "Do not open until Christmas." Sexual intercourse is a gift that says, "Do not open until marriage." If you've already unwrapped it, you can wrap it up again!

Remember, chastity is a *spiritual*, not a physical, state. Chastity is about sexual self-control, an attitude of respect and gratitude for the gift that sex is. Although a person can't regain his or her physical virginity, anyone, *at any time*, can regain chastity. This is often referred to as "secondary virginity." Many, many young people have made the decision to return to chastity.

Living a chaste lifestyle is easier when you keep the advantages of that decision clearly in mind. A 17-year-old girl at an inner-city high school in Washington, D.C. offers this testimony:

Not too long ago when boys asked me if I was a virgin, I was ashamed of it. I'm not anymore. It's better to be a virgin, because boys have more respect for you and you don't have to worry about AIDS tests or pregnancy tests or anything.[2]

A young woman in her 20s adds:

My high school and college years were the best years of my life. I learned that *no* to sex meant *yes* to fun. My reputation as a virgin got out fast. I had more dates, better grades, and good, quality friendships. Guys knew they didn't have to perform (sexually) for me, so we could concentrate on getting to know each other and having a great time.[3]

What are some other advantages of a chaste lifestyle? Many of the advantages have to do with freedom—the freedom of a lifestyle that chastity relieves you *from* and the freedom of a lifestyle that chastity opens you *to*. For example, chastity gives you freedom *from*:

- guilt, doubt, worry, and regret,

- having to wonder, "How far will I go with this person on this date?"

- being used by others and using other people,

- sexually transmitted diseases and (for girls) the possibility of not being able to bear a child because of an STD,

- pregnancy,

- having to choose between raising a child you aren't ready for and giving up your baby for adoption,

- the trauma of abortion,

- loss of reputation,

- pressure to marry early or to marry the wrong person,

- the ghosts of past sexual relationships invading your marriage.

Also, chastity gives you freedom *to*:

- exercise control over your life,

- develop real friendships based on mutual respect shared thoughts, and feelings,

- develop skills, talents, and interests,

- have many relationships,

- develop self-respect and self-control,

- finish your education and achieve financial stability before having to marry,

- find a potential mate who values you for the person you are,

- enjoy greater trust in marriage (because you don't have to worry, "Is he/she going to fool around with someone else, the way we fooled around before we were married?"),

- stay out of sexual sin and grow in your relationship with God.

You may be able to think of still other advantages of leading a chaste life? As you create a vision for your life and future, you surely won't want it to be associated with premarital sex. Only in maintaining or regaining your chastity can you be assured of becoming the person that you—and God—intend for you to be.

Chapter 16

How Can I Be Chaste?

Chastity is not something like a jacket that you can put on or take off whenever you like. Chastity is a part of yourself that communicates itself to others in your daily words and actions.

Modesty, or moderation, is a way to express chastity. Wearing appropriate and non-suggestive clothing, not calling undue attention to your body, and keeping your speech free of sexually suggestive talk are simple ways to let others know what you believe.

In this chapter, we'll share some other strategies for living a chaste lifestyle in a world full of sexual temptations and pressures.

Sex Education

One help is a sex education course that presents all of the advantages of chastity. Fortunately, these courses are beginning to catch on in many schools.

An example is a course that was started by a high school teacher, Coleen Kelly Mast, and six high school students from McNamara High School in Bradley, Illinois. They call themselves the MASH team—McNamara Ambassadors for Sexual Health—and they go around to other schools doing skits that show common situations teenagers have to deal with in the area of sex.

For example, the following dialogue illustrates a girl's response to a guy who is pressuring to have sex:

Guy: But Jody, we love each other ... isn't it natural to show it. It'll bring us closer.

Girl: If we can't get closer by getting to know each other's hearts and minds, sex will never do it. Besides, it's wrong and I'm not going to argue with you about it.

Guy: Don't give me that stuff. I know you want to. Don't worry, I won't hurt you.

Girl: Sex is not a game, and we don't even know the hurts that are involved. Stop playing games with my emotions.

Guy: Don't you *care* about me?

Girl: I care enough to say no, and to forget you ever asked the question.

Some of these skits are shown on a videotape prepared by Coleen Kelly Mast's educational organization called Respect Incorporated. The course itself is called "Sex Respect."[1]

Does a sex education course that promotes chastity really affect teenager's sexual attitudes and behavior? Results show that students who take the course have a lower rate of sexual activity compared to those who take sex education courses that do not advocate chastity. Students who take the Sex Respect course are more likely to agree with statements such as, "There are many benefits to saving sex for marriage."

If you have the opportunity to take a course of this kind it would be beneficial to do so. If you are enrolled in a conventional sex education course that does not advocate chastity, make sure to be a discerning participant. Carefully analyze what is presented to you. Balance the information with what you have learned and believe about chastity.

Ways to Say No

As Molly Kelly says, "You say 'No' before you ever go out on a date. 'No' is in the mind; it's a definite decision."

She points out that there are three kinds of language: verbal language, body language, and clothes language. For "No" to mean "No," all three types of language must be saying it at the same time. For example:

A girl can say no with words, but her tight skirt and skimpy blouse are saying yes. She can say no with her lips, but if her eyes are saying yes, it won't work. A boy can say no while his hands are asking for a yes.[2]

Another piece of advice is to "Advertise yourself, not your sexiness." Of course some young people *want* to be sexy and provocative. In *Sex: It's Worth Waiting For*, youth minister Greg Speck comments:

Women have said to me, "Oh, I just love it when guys lust after me. It's so exciting!"

If that's your reaction, then you don't understand what goes on in the mind of a man. When a man lusts after you, you become a piece of meat! He could care less that you have hopes and dreams and desires. All he wants to do is get his hands on your body.[3]

Lusting is not a complimentary term. Speck goes on to offer specific advice to young women:

Look good, be stylish, but don't compromise yourself as a woman. Stay away from tight jeans, dresses slit up the side, short skirts, halter tops, low-cut tops, sleeveless sweaters with big underarms....

Put on your outfit, stand in the mirror, and ask yourself, "What am I trying to draw attention to?" If it's just your exterior, then in many cases you are going to be treated like a piece of meat.[4]

Modesty in dress, speech, and action is a virtue that applies to everybody, men as well as women. Thomas Lorimer, in his book *Why Not? Why Is Premarital Sex Wrong?* directs similar words of advice to young men:

Guys, decide you will not violate the personal space of any woman. Make a covenant with your eyes not to look at the private parts of women.

Then date only those girls who demonstrate that they are not confused about personal space. Date those who dress modestly. And dress modestly yourself.[5]

How do you say no with words? Saying no often requires more than a one-word answer. It's important to be psychologically prepared for the "lines" that someone may use to pressure you to have sex. Remember, a line demands a comeback that can put an end to the pressure once and for all and really communicate your strong "No."

Here are some comebacks for some of the standard lines:

"Don't you love me?"

"I love you enough to say no."

"If you really loved me, you would."

"If you really loved me, you wouldn't ask. If you really care about somebody, you don't pressure them to do something they don't want to do."

"Everybody's doing it."

"Everybody but *me*."

"Really, everybody's doing it."

"Then you shouldn't have any trouble finding somebody else."

"Don't you find me attractive?"

"I find you very attractive. I like you a lot. That's why I don't want to wreck our relationship by getting too physical."

"I'll stop whenever you say."

"How about right now?"

"I *love* you."

"Then please prove it by respecting my values."

"What are you waiting for."

"I'm waiting for the person I'll marry."

"Are you repressed or something?"

"No, I'm free—from the pressure to have sex before I get married."

| "Sex isn't a big deal." | "It's a big deal to me, a big deal to my future husband (wife), and a big deal to God—and I made a promise that I would wait." |

Although girls can and do often lead guys on, in our experience guys are more likely to use these kinds of lines to get sex. And, sadly, many a girl has fallen for them. A girl may find it hard to believe that a boy is lying when he says, seemingly with great sincerity, "I love you!"

If you're a girl, you need to know two things: (1) If a boy puts *any* kind of pressure on you to go farther than you want to go, it shows he loves *himself*, not you; he's interested only in his pleasure, and he'll sacrifice your self-respect and physical safety to get it; and (2) many guys will lie through their teeth, say anything, and do whatever else they have to do to get sex. Here is one guy who openly admits this:

I learned to maneuver my opponent into a position where she couldn't say no. If I sensed there was a moral dilemma in her mind, I would play any role necessary to reach the point where sex became inevitable.[6]

Rehearse your lines and dress the part (modestly). Learn how to say "No" with your body, words, and behavior.

Dating Strategies

"Dating" is the expression to describe time that guys and girls share together. In this century dating has become a common way for guys and girls to build friendships. For adults, dating is a way for men and women to meet and get to know prospective marriage partners.

However, dating is also the likely occasion for sexual temptations and sexual behavior to occur. As with other areas of your life that are important, it's important to have a strategy and develop guidelines for dating. Here are a few:

1. *Begin with group dating.* Group dating may mean going out with several friends, both guys and girls. Everyone knows everyone else. Nobody is paired off. In another form of group dating, you go out with one person but are accompanied by several friends. Group dating is a good way to begin. It relieves a lot of the pressures of starting a conversation, deciding what to do—and being "alone," when sexual temptations are more likely to arise.

2. *Delay and minimize single dating.* A single date is a guy and girl going out together as a couple. A Brigham Young University study found that the earlier young people began single dating, the more likely they were to lose their virginity by the time of high school graduation. Ninety-one percent of girls who began single dating at age 12 lost their virginity by the time they graduated from high school. Only 20% of girls who started single dating at age 16 lost theirs. Even when you are college-aged, it's best to spend most of your social time in group activity—either group dating or with a circle of friends.

3. *Plan your date.* When you do go on a single date, don't just get together and make it up as you go along. If a date ends up with "nothing to do," it's very easy to get physically involved.

If you run out of things to do, either end the date right then or go to a place where there are other people (at a restaurant, for example). Don't go parking unless you're looking for a struggle with temptation or pressure.

4. *Involve your parents.* You should talk over with at least one of your parents your dating habits—especially when a serious relationship is developing. Doing so will enable you to get the perspective and wisdom of someone who cares about you and your future. If you're not comfortable talking with your parents about the person you're dating, chances are good that you shouldn't be involved with that person.

Also, you should bring your date to your home to meet your parents before you go out. Says one college female: "I think it's really important to get your parents' blessing on a relationship."

5. *Set physical limits.* For example, if you're at home with your date, spend time talking and getting to know the other person. Instead of sitting on the sofa, go sit at the kitchen table and talk while you share a snack. Don't lie on the floor watching TV. Definitely don't sit around in your pajamas watching TV. Needless to say, staying chaste also means avoiding places like parked cars and dormitory rooms.

6. *Avoid sexual stimuli.* Movies with sex scenes, suggestive musical lyrics, and any kind of pornography should be avoided—especially when you are on a date.

7. *Don't drink or use drugs.* Alcohol and other drugs can lower sexual inhibitions; either will make you more likely to give in to sexual temptations.

Avoid parties where there's drinking. In college, where guys and girls may be away from home and their parents' rules for the first time, parties with drinking and drugs are often responses to this new freedom. This "on the edge" behavior also can lead guys and girls to try sex. Girls beware: There are many older college guys waiting for you to drink more alcohol than you can handle so that they can more easily get you to have sex. Many a freshman girl has lost her virginity during the first weekend on campus when some guy got her drunk at a beer party.

Given the dangers of the sex-and-alcohol scene, we would advise guys, but especially young women, *not to drink at all*—unless you are in a protected situation, such as a family gathering.

8. Set strict limits on your expression of physical affection.
Closed-mouth kissing and hugs are usually appropriate ways to express your physical affection. However, any expression that causes genital arousal should be avoided. When you set strict limits, you won't find yourself fighting the temptation to go "a little bit farther" the next time you're together.

9. Go slow.
Don't let intense emotions build too fast. Don't ever ask the other person, "How do you feel about me?" That will artificially accelerate things. Don't talk about "our relationship" and "our future," a mistake many couples today are prone to make. Put up with a little suspense about these things.

You don't have to know everything the person you are dating feels. Let the relationship unfold naturally; you'll have more fun if you keep it light. The respect you show for the person will show how you feel.

Practical Advice

Recently, we were able to interview a group of college students who have made a chastity commitment, to find out what practical advice they would give to others who want to stay chaste in a world full of sexual pressures and dangers. Here are some of things they said:

Tim: Don't get involved with someone who is sexually experienced. That happened to me in high school. She said sex didn't have to be part of our relationship, but it created a subtle pressure. I always felt as if I was disappointing her. Now I wouldn't involve myself with someone whose convictions about how far to go are different from mine.

Once you get involved in sexual activity at all, you'll go farther than you want to go—maybe not right away, but eventually. There's an old saying, "Sin will take you farther than you want to go, and keep you longer than you wanted to stay." So don't even get started.

Rachel: I believe that every person has a different point for self-control. You have to be obedient to your own convictions, what you can handle. And you have to be really honest to keep from falling. You can't fool yourself, and you have to be willing to discuss this issue with your partner.

La Chauna: If the other person is putting *any* pressure on you, be very explicit about your standards. Know your boundaries before you are with the person, and stick to your guns!

Eun Gyeong: Get to know the other person. Find out how they feel about certain things. Don't start dating someone until you feel you are already friends with them. If somebody pressures you to "go out," definitely don't.

Grace: When you do go out, don't talk too much about yourself. That can lead the other person on. Keep the focus on other things—things you have in common.

Hugo: You might want to be alone, but don't. If your parents aren't home, for example, you'll be tempted to be alone. But don't—the temptation is too much.

Tim: Always keep the door open!

Choosing Friends Who Share Your Values

It's vital to have friends who share your values concerning chastity. A study by the Institute for Research and Evaluation found that teens who had friends who promised to abstain from premarital sex were significantly more likely to remain chaste than teens who did not have supportive friends.

Sandra Hill, a mother and community health nurse, says that at her daughter's high school, small groups of girls are pledging to each other not to have sex.

"All it takes is one supportive friend to say, 'I'm not going to do that.' And others will say, 'Well, I'm not going to do that either.' My own daughter and five friends vowed to each other to remain virgins while they were in high school, and they all did it."

Just as bad company corrupts good character, good company builds it up. Aristotle said, "The brave are found where the brave are honored." The same is true for chastity.

Having And Keeping Your High Standards

A woman came to our college campus to speak on the subject of date rape. She had dinner with a small group of women students before her talk.

"Does a guy here think he has a right to sex if he has spent money on you?" she asked.

One of the young women said, "Guys here expect sex if they just *pay attention* to you."

The really sad thing is that guys not only expect this; many of them get it. Why? One reason is that there are many girls (and guys) who do not value themselves very highly.

Said a woman student: "You have to value yourself as a person and value your body."

Girls often ask, "What if the guy really seems to care about me?" Remember, if he really cares, he won't pressure you to have sex. And if a young woman gives in to pressure for sex so as not to lose him, it shows she values the imagined relationship more than she does her own importance. Her sense of self-worth is not very great.

If a girl loses a guy because she wouldn't give in, she is well to be rid of him. Here's the story of a 16-year-old girl who had that happened to her:

I was very naive about sex (the only information I was able to get was from booklets and listening to friends). I had the usual crushes on boys who didn't notice me. My ninth grade year, though, I found out what it's like to stand up for your morals.

The first kiss was not all that enjoyable and the hands up the shirt shocked me. The next time we were alone, the boy tried to go all the way. After I said no and explained my position, he took me home in complete silence. I was hurt when he no longer wanted to see me, but I was confident I had done the right thing.[7]

Waiting for the Right Person

Some young women and men have sex because they're so worried about having and keeping a boyfriend or girlfriend or getting someone to marry them that they'll do anything to try to hold on to that partner. What they need is the kind of confidence expressed by a young woman who spoke at a church discussion on sex, dating, and chastity that we participated in:

I used to be on the hunt—thinking I had to be where guys were and to make myself available if I was going to find a husband. Eventually, I realized I was not trusting God in this matter. So I began praying, "Lord, please find me a mate, if that is your will for me, and help me trust in your providence."

I stopped chasing guys. And in less than a year, I met my future husband, a wonderful man—the one I believe God had picked out for me all along.

Having high standards also means being willing to go without dates—or a mate—until someone comes along who meets those standards.

That's not easy. A friend, whose oldest daughter is a senior in college, said to us recently: "Rebecca called the other night. She's very down. Just about all the girls she knows are sleeping with their boyfriends. She's beginning to despair of ever finding a boy who shares her belief in chastity."

We sympathize with young people who are in that situation. One very helpful way we suggest to help support your decision to remain chaste is to continue to read books which promote it.

We have listed some recommended books in the appendix at the end of this book. Every author comes at the subject in a little different way and all are valuable. Every author includes his or her own sample of success and failure stories which are very motivating when your resolve to remain chaste may be at a low ebb. Reading books of this kind is a way to help counteract the continual barrage of sexually permissive messages that are all around you. We think you will be amazed at the difference this makes in your confidence and your resolve.

One such book we believe is helpful is Julia Duin's *Purity Makes the Heart Grow Stronger: Sexuality and the Single Christian.* Julia Duin is a single young adult in her twenties. She writes in a very personal and positive way about how she goes about living out her commitment to chastity. Duin shares the story of a man—a fellow Christian reporter—"who told me that the first few choices to abstain from premarital sex were the most difficult for him." She adds:

But after he set a pattern of saying no, he grew more used to refusing. He hardened himself to teasing from people. Then someone tried to seduce him at a party. What made him fight her off were the choices he had made. He had invested so much in keeping his sexual purity, he saw no reason to give it up on a whim.

As you think about and look for the kind of person you'd like to marry, also keep this in mind: A successful marriage requires good character. If someone is selfish, rude, unappreciative, lazy, ill-tempered, or dishonest now, don't count on her or him to change after you're married. As you date a person (one you're getting serious about), ask yourself:

- How does he/she treat me?

- How does he/she treat other people?

- Will this person be a good role model for my children?

- Will this person be someone I would be proud to call my husband or wife?

If the person comes up short on questions like these, don't waste time on that relationship.

The best way to find the sort of person you'd like to marry is to *become that kind of person yourself.* Whatever qualities you admire in other people, strive to develop them in yourself. Develop your own character. Develop your gifts, your talents, and your interests. If you focus on improving yourself instead of trying to put yourself in situations where you might meet Mr. or Ms. Right, you'll become the attractive person—more likely to attract the kind of person you'd be willing to spend your life with.

With God's Help

Our last recommendation for maintaining your chastity is this: Don't try to do it without God.

"Definitely stay in prayer," said Joe, one of the college students we interviewed. "Ask God to help you know your limits."

Added Hugo: "It takes a lot of prayer. You have to pray that your relationships will not in any way violate God's laws. The important thing is knowing God's standards and trying to keep them."

Rachel reminded us that God knows we're not perfect and that we can come to God for forgiveness when we slip: "If you do fall from your convictions, don't think you're a hypocrite. Get right back up. Just say to yourself, 'I've got to keep trying to live up to godly standards.' Don't let anyone tell you there's no forgiveness."

Growing numbers of young people are also helping themselves stay chaste by making a formal promise to God. Many, for example, are taking part in a national campaign called "True Love Waits." The pledge goes like this:

Believing that true love waits, I make a commitment to God, myself, those I date, my future mate, and my future children to be sexually pure until the day I enter a covenant marriage relationship.

Joshua, 15, took the pledge. He says: "Whenever I get in a situation where I'm tempted, I remember it. I consider it a sacred thing. It's enough to keep me from going through with something I would regret."

Says Traci, a college freshman: "I don't have a boyfriend yet, but I have written a sealed letter to my future husband telling him that I love him enough to wait. I am very excited about the prospect of God having someone for me."

We want to close this chapter by addressing those of you who may have lost your virginity. You may be feeling bad about that and thinking, "It's too late for me." It's not. Don't be discouraged. God doesn't want you to dwell on past mistakes, which we all make.

You can choose now to follow chastity as your future path. You can recapture all the freedom and other benefits of chastity. Writes Pat Driscoll:

Most people who have struggled to bring chastity into their lives after a period of sexual indulgence report a remarkable inner peace. The struggle may bring fearful conflict, but if the individual perseveres in chastity for several months or a year, he or she will experience an almost spontaneous sense of integration.[8]

God will bless you for this decision and give you abundant grace to carry it out. Help yourself by leaving behind old relationships that involved sex. Ask God's help every day in prayer. God won't let you down.

Chapter 17

What Can I Look Forward To?

I, Mark, take you, Lisa, for my wife, to have and to hold, from this day forward, for better, for worse, for richer, for poorer, in sickness and in health, until death do us part.

I, Lisa, take you, Mark, for my husband, to have and to hold, from this day forward, for better, for worse, for richer, for poorer, in sickness and in health, until death do us part.

Let's suppose you've saved sex for marriage. Or, if you lost your virginity, you've chosen secondary virginity, the moral and spiritual commitment to practice chastity in the future and wait for your marriage partner.

What can you look forward to once you *are* married (if that's the vocation in life God calls you to)?

A Christian marriage will be a total yes to your beloved. Because of commitment, marriage is the place where sex belongs, where it means what it's supposed to mean. Sex in marriage is a physical union which signifies a couple's total union.

In the first months and years of marriage, sex is likely to be quite a frequent event. As time goes on, each couple develops their own pattern of lovemaking. Whatever the pattern, your sex life will be best when both you and your marriage partner put the other first, seeking to please the other in love.

Mark, age 26, and Lisa, age 24, have been married for two-and-a-half years. They are expecting their first child. We asked them to share their thoughts about sex in marriage. Lisa started out by saying, "I think we have a great sex life!"

But she added this note of realism: "Anyone who gets married and thinks they're going to have sex every night for the rest of their lives is not living in the real world.

"And that doesn't just mean couples who have ten kids and are always too worn out by the time they go to bed. People also have jobs, they have school, they have other commitments.

Lisa continued:

Coming into marriage you have to trust that what's important is the quality of the lovemaking, not the quantity. It really is true that one fantastic night is better than ten when you're exhausted."

Mark commented: "Lisa's point is a good one. Sex is an essential part of marriage, but it isn't the *reason* for marriage. You don't get married in order to have sex. You get married in order to be united to another person."

Lisa added: "And you *get* to have sex, which is really a nice thing!"

The Secret of a Happy Marriage

Sex is a very good part of married life, but it is only part of a larger picture. We'd like to take a closer look at this larger view and see how sex fits in.

A young wife wrote to a priest who writes an advice column:

Dear Padre,
   I want my marriage to last and my family to be happy. What is the secret?

—Pauline

The priest's answer was simple. He said that the happiness of the husband and wife depended on *how they treated each other*. Then he went on to cite several key qualities that have been found to foster genuine love, intimacy, and friendship between marriage partners. Here are some of the most important qualities:

1. *Equal power.* Happily married couples work hard to make decisions *together*. They respect the other person's point of view. They try not to dominate each other.

We know couples whose marriages very much lack this kind of equality and shared decision-making. Often it is the husband who calls the shots. The wife, who often isn't even consulted on these things, typically gets even by complaining about his decisions both before and after.

A basic rule for married life is this (and we can't emphasize this too strongly): *Get the consent of the other person.*

You can practice this shared decision-making now with your boyfriend or girlfriend (or in other friendships). Make the effort to decide things together (what to do on a date, for example), instead of either making the decision yourself or just going along with what the other person wants to do.

2. Commitment. Research reveals that commitment is another key to a happy marriage. Commitment in marriage means putting your relationship with your husband or wife before all others. Everything (but God) comes second to the protection and happiness of your spouse.

This means that your husband or wife is more important than your softball league or your friends. Your partner's happiness is more important than your work or career. Your spouse is even more important than your children.

We've seen marriages slowly fall apart when the husband and wife's relationship takes a back seat to something or someone else.

For example, Frank considered himself a good provider and a good father. But he neglected his wife, Carol. He divided his time at home among the kids, the work he had brought home, and watching sports on TV. (Television, believe it or not, is a great danger to a marriage; hours of potential communication and interaction between a husband and wife are lost while one or the other stares at a TV screen.) Carol understood the problem and asked Frank to take walks with her each evening after dinner. He did it for a week and then lost interest. Carol felt devalued and unloved as a person and as a wife, and became even more lonely and unhappy in their marriage.

Putting your spouse first is one part of what commitment in marriage entails. The second part of commitment is permanence. Permanence is expressed in the wellknown words "till death do us part."

Millions of marriages end in divorce (though, we're happy to say, the divorce rate is now beginning to decline). Divorce creates deep pain for both spouses and children. You may have experienced the heartache of divorce first-hand.

How can you avoid the pain of divorce when you get married? One way is to eliminate the *possibility* of divorce. For example, don't go into marriage thinking, "If this doesn't work out, we'll just get divorced." Having divorce as a possibility in your mind definitely increases the likelihood that you'll use that "escape hatch" when the going gets tough. And periodically, it does.

Dr. Clifford Swensen, a psychologist at Purdue University, surveyed thousands of people over his 30-year career in an effort to determine the meaning of love. His conclusion was that love is *not* romance. True love is commitment. He explains:

Romance may bring people together, but commitment is what sustains their love. Romantic love is time-limited, because it's based in part on illusions.

When reality intrudes—after the honeymoon, for example—*believing* that marriage is permanent is what replaces romance with love.

If you *act* as if marriage is permanent, you'll begin feeling that way, too. There's a principle in psychology: If you behave in a certain way, your feelings will follow.[1]

Ralph Martin, in his book *Husbands, Wives, Parents, Children,* confirms this power of believing in the permanence of marriage:

> Scripture teaches that God wants the unity of husband and wife to remain unbroken. I have seen marriages change completely [improve for the better] once the partners understood that their love was not at the whim of their feelings, but rested on a *decision* they made.

This decision is in fact the solemn promise that a couple makes to one another in their marriage vows. (Did you know that on your wedding day you promise to stay with your spouse for life, no matter what?)

We have two good friends who have been married for 18 years. They have five children. They have gone through some very hard times together, financially and emotionally.

The husband says:

> Love in marriage means having that rockbottom sense of permanence. If you don't have that, every fight could be the end, every disagreement will cause you to think, "How can we get through this?"
>
> But you don't just chuck it. You get through the disagreements. Sometimes it takes more than 24 hours. But there is a peace that comes from the sacramental commitment to permanence.

His wife adds: "I would say to young couples, do not be afraid of your struggles. Embrace them together. And both partners must practice sacrificial love—putting the happiness of the other before their own."

Don't assume you can make a certain plan for your life and things will smoothly follow that path. If you do you may be setting yourself up for frustration and disappointment. Saying "yes" to your beloved means opening yourself to an adventure. Where will your life together lead? What struggles will you face? What joys will you share? The very meaning of the word sacrament is "mystery." Marriage is an *ongoing* sacrament in which God will lead you and your spouse on a lifelong journey. On that journey you can experience the depth of committed, faithful, and unselfish love.

Sex is a great part of this journey. In the security of a permanent and committed relationship, a person's enjoyment of sex can only grow.

In *Making a Marriage*, authors Kevin and Marilyn Ryan write:

Sex is a learned behavior. To be good at sex, to enjoy it fully, takes skill.

Some people initially may have more talent or interest than others, but that changes. We learn about our own bodies and our partners' bodies. We learn what they like and need, and what we like and need. We learn how to establish a mood, how to respond to the other.

Making love, like making a marriage, takes time and practice.

3. Sharing. Happily married couples do a lot of sharing. They share interests, activities, friends, thoughts, feelings, and faith.

One-on-one time is an important part of this sharing. In a marriage, it creates feelings of intimacy, of closeness. Intimacy—not the physical need for sex—is the deepest human need. And when emotional intimacy is present in your marriage, sexual intimacy will be much better.

John and Kathy Colligan, in their book *The Healing Power of Love*, describe various kinds of emotionally intimate lovemaking they've experienced as a married couple; these are beautiful examples of ways that sexual love strengthen and sweeten a marriage. They explain:

Sometimes, in making love, we communicate our feelings of celebration. We've just had a great day or a romantic evening. Then we're saying, "Wow, isn't life great!"

When one of us has had a terrible day at work, or has been the victim of criticisms or complaints, our lovemaking says, "I believe in you. You are wonderful to me."

Sometimes we have made love after an argument—even when we didn't feel like it. Then our lovemaking soothes away the leftover hard feelings.... We come away thinking the issue is not so important—not as long as we love each other.

In times of pain and deep emotional crisis, when all we want to do is curl up in a corner and shrink away from one another, our lovemaking draws us outward into the loving reality of one another's bodies.[2]

Clearly, the sharing of the gift of sex between a husband and wife is a way to enhance intimacy—emotional, intellectual, spiritual, and physical intimacy. Sex, however, is not the only way to foster intimacy in a relationship. At a family reunion, a couple—happily married for 42 years—were asked by younger family members (some of whose marriages had not lasted), "What's your secret?"

The wife answered: "Every night—no matter how our day has gone, how tired we are, or whether or not we have argued—we fall asleep holding hands."

That's the sense of intimacy that holds a marriage together, long after one person's hair has thinned and the other has gained extra weight. Even before marriage you can cultivate this deeper sense of intimacy in your close relationships. You can share with others—in words and actions—what you value, what you believe in, who you really are.

4. Trust. What leads some husbands or wives to cheat on their spouse? Sometimes it is an unhappy marriage that causes a person to seek attention, affirmation, and sexual love outside of their marriage. Other times it is purely the case of one person giving into sexual temptation. Married people experience sexual temptations and opportunities as single people do. When you are married, you have to be prepared to resist them.

One way to avoid infidelity is to remember your marriage vows. A husband says that he remembers the sacredness of his promises every time he looks at his wedding ring. Another way is to imagine the terrible pain that infidelity causes. Even if a person's cheating is never found out by his or her spouse, the guilt that results from the experience will become a serious barrier to future intimacy between the couple.

You can begin now to become a trustworthy person, the kind your friends can absolutely rely on to be truthful in what you say and to carry through on what you say you're going to do. You can begin to develop the character trait of self-control that comes from saying no to the sexual temptations you encounter.

5. Forgiveness and Reconciliation.
In marriage, the skills of forgiveness and reconciliation are absolutely essential. Forgiveness can lead to a repair or reconciliation of the relationship that, left unmended, may not be able to grow.

Nearly every day there will be things you will have to forgive your spouse for. Sometimes these are little things—like failing to leave enough hot water for the next person's shower. Sometimes these are bigger things—like making plans for the evening without consulting the other. Regardless, it's important to clear the air. If you don't forgive and let go of hurts, resentment will build and eventually poison your marriage.

Forgiveness leads to reconciliation. Studies show that healthy marriages and families have adopted formulas or "reconciliation rituals" to help people make up quickly after hurting the other or being hurt themselves.

In our marriage, we've cleared the air by asking the other for "a hug for health" (a ritual that one of our children originally suggested). If it's the case of an argument over something silly or ridiculous, we sometimes literally "wipe the slate clean" by pretending it never happened.

Occasionally anger threatens to overwhelm any kind of rational communication in a marriage. There will be times when you'll be so mad at the other person that you'll feel like throwing something or storming out the door and taking off.

Recipe For A Happy Marriage

1 cup of consideration

1 cup of courtesy

2 cups of flattery carefully concealed

2 cups of milk of human kindness

1 gallon faith in God and each other

2 cups of praise

1 reasonable budget

a generous dash of cooperation

CHILDREN

1 large or several small hobbies

1 cup of blindness to the other's faults

Flavor with frequent portions of recreation and a dash of happy memories. Stir well and remove any specks of jealousy, temper, or criticism. Sweeten well with generous portions of love and keep warm with a steady flame of devotion.

Never serve with a cold shoulder or a hot tongue.

—Father Camillus Barth, C.P.

At moments like this, you think, "*I'm* not going to be the one to make up—not when *she's* (*he's*) so clearly in the wrong!"

Remember these rules: (1) be willing to forgive and accept forgiveness, and (2) initiate a reconciliation, *regardless* of who you think is in the wrong. *This is hard to do, but you must do it.* The sooner the reconciliation takes place, the sooner you will be able to move forward in your relationship.

7. Prayer. We attended a wedding recently where the minister exhorted the couple to make Christ the center of their marriage. To do that, he said, you must pray. You must keep Jesus present in your marriage and call on him to help you, *especially* when misunderstanding and conflict occur.

The minister said we all know how common divorce has become. But he pointed out that a current study found that for married couples who went to church together every week, the divorce rate was only 1 in 40. For couples who prayed together every day, the divorce rate was only 1 in 400.

Daily prayer—both shared prayer and individual prayer—helps a couple be more kind, more patient, and more forgiving with one other. Prayer also opens us to be channels of God's grace and love. And time with God is a great way to reduce the stress that is part of any marriage and family. Once again, you can practice this now, learning to rely on prayer as a source of strength and healing in your current relationships with friends and family.

Marriage and Children

For most married couples, the most satisfying, worthwhile, and fulfilling work of life is raising a family. When most people look back on their lives in their later years, they count as little the money they made, the power they wielded, or the pleasures they enjoyed. What matters most is the love that surrounds them.

Both to provide a couple with love and happiness that a family brings and to sustain the human race, God designed sexual love in marriage to be fruitful: to bring forth children. This is sometimes called God's "two-in-one" plan for sex: Married lovemaking has the double purpose of expressing love between the partners and creating new life.

To appreciate God's two-in-one plan for sex in marriage we need to contrast it with the one-dimensional view of sex that much of the world has.

Many, if not most, people today associate sex only with pleasure and with *avoiding* pregnancy and birth. They think of sex as something you can have with anyone, anytime. People who are having sex outside of marriage, for example, will look for ways to make sure that sex doesn't result in pregnancy.

But God's plan intends for sex to be both for the expression of love *and* for the procreation of children. God intended for these two purposes to be inseparable. That's one big reason why God places sex within marriage. Marriage is right place where a couple can give themselves to one another totally—emotionally, spiritually, socially, and physically. Marriage is also the right place for a couple to conceive and raise a child.

Children have been called the "supreme gift" and "ultimate crown" of married life. As part of the marriage vows, couples are asked if they "will accept children lovingly from God, and bring them up according to the law of Christ and the church." To disconnect sex and children—to separate sexual love from its God-given power to create new life—is to go against God's design.

Natural Family Planning

Although the Catholic church teaches that God designs sex to bring forth children, it also recognizes the right of married couples to plan their families while always remaining prayerfully open to God's will and to the possibility of an unexpected pregnancy. The church is not unreasonable; it permits couples to take into account issues like income, health, and ability to care for children.

Responsible parenting covers a wide spectrum. It means a willingness to accept children if a pregnancy unexpectedly occurs. It means putting children and raising a family before things like convenience, career advancement, or material possessions. It means thinking of children as a blessing, a gift from God—and being willing to raise all the children that God blesses you with. In means, in short, that God's plan for your life is the best plan.

The church prohibits the use of artificial contraceptives to prevent pregnancy. (Artificial contraceptives use some sort of artificial device—such as the pill, diaphragm, a spermicide, or condom—to block conception.) The church supports the use of Natural Family Planning (NFP) as a method of responsible parenting. While approving NFP, the church also stresses that it must never be abused—that is, never used by a couple to avoid pregnancy without a just reason.

How does NFP work? Through daily examination of the color and thickness of a woman's cervical mucus, she can determine the days of her fertility cycle when she is likely to get pregnant. Most married couples who practice NFP keep a chart that displays the days of the woman's cycle. After checking her mucus, the woman will note whether or not the day is suitable for intercourse—depending on whether or not she and her husband are trying to have a child, or trying to postpone a pregnancy.

If a wife and a husband were trying to have a baby, they would want to be sure to have intercourse during the fertile days. If they were trying—for good reasons—to avoid having a baby, then they would abstain from having intercourse during the woman's fertile period.

"Holy cow," you may be thinking. "You mean I not only have to abstain from sex *before* I'm married, but *after* I'm married, too?"

Of course abstaining does require self-control. But besides being an effective form of delaying pregnancy (up to 98% effective if practiced correctly), many married couples who practice NFP actually say that it *improves* their sex lives.

We asked Mark and Lisa about this. "Can your sex life be as good as a couple's who use artificial contraception and can therefore have sex whenever they please?"

"Absolutely—better!" Lisa answered.

SEX, LOVE, AND YOU

"Better, better," Mark added. "Because abstaining makes the times you do get together so much more of an event."

Other couples have shared how knowing, at the beginning of a day, that they are in the right part of the woman's cycle to have intercourse has heightened the anticipation of sex, given the couple something to look forward to all day, and improved their communication in other areas. Also, just as fasting from food helps people to really appreciate food when the fast is over, abstaining from sex for a few days likewise sharpens a couple's appreciation of sex, too.

"People say you miss a certain spontaneity, and there have been nights when we wished we could be spontaneous, but it's never been an overbearing feeling for us," said Lisa.

There are also other rewards of Natural Family Planning. Lisa explains:

> Sexual intercourse is meant to be an act of complete self-giving. But if you use artificial contraception, you're not giving yourself completely. You're holding back your procreative potential. It's as if you're saying, "I give myself totally, but I really don't."

Mark adds:

> When you're obeying the natural order in this way—leaving every sexual union open to the possibility of life— you're also more open to the call of God, to the prompting that it's time to have a baby.

After two-and-a-half years of using NFP to postpone pregnancy, Mark and Lisa began to feel a stronger readiness to start a family. They began to have intercourse at times when Lisa was likely fertile. Soon they were expecting a child.

(For complete, "how to" information on NFP, see: *The Art of Natural Family Planning*, available from the Couple to Couple League, P.O. Box 11184, Cincinnati, OH 45211; 513-661-7612.)

Looking Back: Why It's Right to
Save Sex for Marriage

When you were younger, your parents or some other adult may have often told you about something they found hard to explain with words like, "You'll just have to wait and see" or "You'll understand when you're older."

We hope that we've given you plenty of good reasons why chastity before marriage is the right decision—beneficial to who you are now and who you will become in the future. But understanding completely why it's important to practice chastity now is something you may not fully understand until you are married. Lisa said, "Before Mark and I got married, our sexuality weighed heavily on me, as I think it does on other young couples. We loved each other so much...."

She paused and continued:

> But once I was married, it was clear to me why we
> waited, much clearer than it was before we got married.
> Now I feel, as a married person, that it's really important
> to tell my single friends that might be struggling that
> once you're married you will understand the incredible
> power that sex has to be a unifying force in your lives.
>
> The truth of this becomes completely clear only when
> your lives are truly unified—when you're sharing the
> same checking account, when you're in the same house,
> when you have to learn to live with this other person in a
> million ways. Sex becomes a real celebration of that unity.
> Before marriage, sex doesn't have that powerful symbolic
> quality to it.

Anyone who is struggling with chastity now, Lisa said, "should have the faith that if you do love this person and you are going to get married, sex is going to be better than you ever dreamed of if you wait."

She offered these final words of caution and encouragement:

I think you will regret it if you give in beforehand. If you wait, the first contact will really be in the context where sex can be as good as God made it to be.

SEX, LOVE, AND YOU

The Secret of Happiness

We started this chapter by talking about the secret of a happy marriage. We'd like to end this chapter—and the book—by talking about the secret of a happy life, whether your vocation is marriage, being single, or the vowed religious life.

A few years ago, there was a popular singer who literally began at the bottom of the career ladder and rose—through many years of hard work—to the top. He had big record sales, his own television program, fame, groupies—everything he thought he always wanted. Once at the top, however, he found himself asking, "Is this all there is?"

He had expected happiness to go along with all the money and fame. Instead, he found emptiness. At the peak of his career, he committed suicide.

The lesson in this man's story is that the most important thing to be gained from this life is not fame, power, money, or sex. The most important thing to learn, to do, to be is love. As Mother Teresa puts it: "We are created to love, and to be loved."

> Love is patient, love is kind. It is not jealous ... it is not rude, it does not seek its own interests, it is not quick-tempered, it does not brood over injury ... It bears all things ... Love never fails.
> —1 Corinthians 13:4-8

If you learn to love at this stage of your life, you will be prepared to enter whatever life vocation you eventually choose. If you can love, you will receive everything you need from life. Jesus said "Love one another as I have loved you" (Jn 13:34). This is not the "love" of popular songs; this is the Christ-like love of sharing and sacrifice. The kind of love that leads a person to spend his or her life in service of others. Loving in this way is the secret of happiness.

May God bless and keep you and grant you every happiness in this life and the next.

Appendix

Further Readings on Chastity—Books

George Eager, *Love, Dating, and Sex: What Teens Want to Know.* 208 pages, $9.95 (add $1.00 per book for shipping). Order directly from Mailbox Club Books, 404 Eager Rd., Valdosta, GA 31602 (1-800-488-5226).

This is a very popular book with teens. It's written in down-to-earth language and filled with practical ideas and true stories you can relate to. Terrific art.

Other books you'll enjoy by George Eager (all of these have excellent art, too):

■ *Peer Pressure.* 144 pages, $5.95. How to take control of your own life and say no to drugs and premarital sex.

■ *Understanding Your Sex Drive.* Includes the "five laws of guy-girl relationships" and secondary virginity.

■ *Love and Dating.* 96 pages, $5.95. Defines three kinds of love and poses the questions "How do you rate with your date?" and "How far is too 'too far'?"

Julia Duin, *Purity Makes the Heart Grow Stronger: Sexuality and the Single Christian,* 150 pages, $7.95. Order from Servant Publishing, P.O. Box 8617, Ann Arbor, MI 48107.

Julia Duin is a Christian news reporter committed to living a chaste lifestyle. She does it, she says, by developing a lot of interests that keep her busy and growing as a person and by seeking a close relationship with Jesus Christ.

Thomas H. Lorimer, *Why Not? Why Is Premarital Sex Wrong?* 131 pages, $4.95. Order from AMG Publishers, 6815 Shallowford Rd., Chattanooga, TN 37422.

A very fast read, this book includes simple, straightforward chapters on the many negative outcomes of premarital sex, including its negative effects on marriage. We believe Mr. Lorimer's original slant and his keen observations of human behavior.

Joe. S. McIlhaney, Jr. M.D., *Sexuality and Sexually Transmitted Diseases.* 167 pages. Baker Book House, P. O. Box 6287, Grand Rapids, MI 49516.

Dr. McIlhaney is a gynecologist who specializes in the treatment of infertility. Written in a personal, non-technical style, this book tells of the danger of infertility due to contracting STDs in premarital sexual activity.

Greg Speck, *Sex: It's Worth Waiting For.* 221 pages. Order from Moody Press, 820 N. LaSalle Dr., Chicago IL 60610.

Greg Speck has been a youth minister and has worked with troubled teens. He's a good writer—not boring—and gives excellent tips on the do's and don'ts of dating. He also treats sensitive topics such as incest, rape, masturbation, and homosexuality.

Booklets

Jim Auer, *Responsible Sex: What Every Teen Should Know.* 23 pages, 75 cents. Liguori Publications, P.O. Box 060, Liguori, MO 63057-9999 (1-800-325-9521, Ext. 060).

Presents a logical argument that respectfully and intelligently challenges teens to wait until marriage before having sex.

George Eager, *Save Sex, What Is Real Love?, Dating, Understanding Your Sex Drive, Peer Pressure: How to Handle It,* and *Relationships: How To Be a Winner!* Set of six booklets (each about 25 pages) is $6.00. Order from Mailbox Club Books 404 Eager Rd., Valdosta, GA 31602 (1-800-488-5226).

Molly Kelly, *Chastity: The Only Choice.* 12 pages, 80 cents (70 cents per 100 copies).

A mother of eight, Molly Kelly is a nationally known speaker who speaks annually to more than fifty thousand teens about "saved sex." She writes in a practical, down-to-earth style.

Molly Kelly, *Abortion: Beyond Personal Choice.* 12 pages, 80 cents.

Gives the facts about a baby's development in the womb and the straight facts about abortion. You are urged to take a stand. Adoption is presented as an alternative to abortion that "saves the lives of innocent babies and gives the gift of life to families wanting children."

Order either booklet from The Center for Learning, P.O. Box 910, Villa Maria, PA 16155 (1-800-967-9090).

Joe. S. McIlhaney Jr., M.D. *Why Condoms Aren't Safe.* 14 pages, 35 cents. Focus on the Family, Colorado Springs, CO 80955 (1-800-A-FAMILY).

Dr. McIlhaney tells stories from his personal medical practice to show all the reasons why condoms don't make premarital sex physically safe. A must resource in the debate about "safe sex."

Other first-rate Focus on the Family booklets include:

- *The First Nine Months.* Beautiful photos by Lennart Nelsson of babies in the womb and a description of pre-natal development month-by-month.

- *Why Wait for Marriage,* by Tim Stafford. Tim answers actual letters he received when he wrote about sexuality for *Campus Life* magazine.

- *Sex and Singles: Reasons to Wait,* by Paul C. Reisser, M.D. Good reasons "to wait" are well-presented.

- *How to Help Your Kids Say No to Sex.* Encouragement and suggestions for parents, plus a good list of further resources.

- *Tough Love for Singles,* by Dr. James Dobson. Practical advice for young adults. Suggests what makes people interested in you and what keeps them interested.

- *How One Doctor Changed Her Mind About Abortion,* by Beverly McMillan, M. D. A true story about how Dr. McMillan changed what she believed about abortion.

- *What Does God Say About Abortion?* Questions about abortion answered with scripture quotations.

- *Identifying and Overcoming Post Abortion Syndrome,* by Teri K. Reisser, M. S. and Paul C. Reisser, M. D. Full explanation of PAS illustrated with true stories. Written by a crisis pregnancy counselor and her physician husband. Compassionate and helpful.

Pamphlets

Abortion: Some Medical Facts. 17 cents (15 cents for 100 copies or more). NRL Educational Trust Fund, 419 7th St., N.W., Suite 500, Washington, D.C. 20004 (202-626-8809).

Clear, authoritative explanation of the medical facts on abortion. Overviews six types of abortion, including their medical and psychological complications.

Is Sex Safe? A Look at: Sexually Transmitted Diseases (STDs). 25 cents each for one to nine copies (unit price decreases with larger order). Published by Grapevine Publications, P. O. Box 45057, Boise, Idaho 83711, 1992.

Complete information on STDs. Also includes the advice to save sex for marriage. Inexpensive enough to be passed out liberally.

Sex Outside Marriage ... Why Not? 25 cents (10 cents for 100 copies or more). WOMANITY, 1700 Oak Park Blvd. Annex, Pleasant Hill, CA 94523 (415-943-6424).

Presented in simple panels, this appealing pamphlet clearly explains what's wrong with all the forms of sex outside marriage, including: adultery, homosexual sex, premarital sex, and masturbation.

Other clever and concise pamphlets by WOMANITY include: *How To Say No Without Losing His/Her Love, God's Plan for Sex,* and *Secondary Virginity.*

To Save a Life and *Life Lines: What You Can Do About Abortion.* $4.00 per 100. Christopher News Notes, 12 East 48th Street, New York, NY 10017.

Published by the Catholic group, the Christopher Society, these are two excellent pamphlets that list practical ways to make a positive contribution to pro-life work; also includes resources for women facing crisis pregnancies.

Videos

Abortion Issues. 48 minutes, $24.95. Available from the Center for Learning, P.O. Box 910, Villa Maria, PA 16155 (1-800-967-9090).

A straightforward talk by Molly Kelly. Teens are presented the facts on abortion, including possible medical complications and side effects.

No Second Chance. 30 minutes, $19.95. Available from Jeremiah Films, Dept. B, P.O. Box 1710, Hemet, CA 92343 (800-828-2290).

An emotionally charged film on AIDS and sexual abstinence.

Pro-Life Doctors Speak Out. 17 minutes. Available from American Portrait Films, 503 E. 200 St., Cleveland, OH 44119 (800-736-4567).

Excellent presentation on the medical facts on abortion given by three leading pro-life doctors: Dr. John Wilke, Dr. Bernard Nathanson, and former Surgeon General C. Everett Koop. If you can show only one pro-life film, show this. (We've used this as part of a combined chastity and respect for life presentation to parents and teens.)

Second Thoughts, 28 minutes. Available from Bethany Productions, 901 Eastern Ave. NE, Grand Rapids, MI 49503 (616-459-6273).

A well-made, fast-paced fictional drama featuring a teenage dilemma that portrays the dangers of premarital sex and offers hope and comfort for teens who have been sexually active and want to change.

Sex, Lies, and the Truth, 30 minutes. Available from Focus on the Family, Colorado Springs, CO 80995 (719-531-3400).

A riveting look at the hard truth about the price of sex outside marriage. Includes a strong focus on the danger of AIDS. Comes in two versions, one for public school use, another for Christian settings. The Christian version includes compelling personal testimonies from wellknown figures on how faith helps them stay chaste.

Teens and Chastity. 43 minutes, $29.95. Available from The Center for Learning, P.O. Box 910, Villa Maria, PA 16155 (1-800-967-9090).

Humorous, dynamic presentation by Molly Kelly taped at a public high school assembly. She addresses topics like teen pregnancy, AIDS, the myth of safe sex, and the rewards of chastity.

Your Crisis Pregnancy. $49.95. Available from American Portrait Films, 1695 W. Crescent Ave., Suite 500, Anaheim, CA 92801 (714-535-2189).

A sensitive, hopeful treatment of crisis pregnancy; includes the real-life stories of four women who faced crisis pregnancies and chose life-affirming solutions.

Window to the Womb. Available from Images, VMG, P.O. Box 199, Birmingham, MI 48012 (313-360-0743).

Provides ultrasound footage of early fetal development that shows the power of sex to create new human life. Used in a number of chastity-based sex education programs.

Audiotape

"Sex, Love, and Intimacy," by Dick Purnell. Available from Dick Purnell Ministry, P.O. Box 850846, Richardson, TX 75085 (214-234-0855).

Dick Purnell is funny enough to be a stand-up comic. But after he has you laughing he delivers a clear and compelling message about the dangers of uncommitted sex and the benefits of saving sex for marriage.

Notes

Part I

1. Anonymous quote from *A Community of Caring* (New York: Walker Publishing Co., 1982).

Chapter 1

1. Lou Harris, "American Teens Speak: Sex, Myths, TV, and Birth Control" (poll commissioned by Planned Parenthood of America, 1986).
2. Centers for Disease Control, "Sexual Behaviors Among High School Students, U.S.," reported in *Morbidity and Mortality Weekly Report*, 1992.
3. *Ibid.*
4. National survey by Zelnick and Kanter cited in W. Kilpatrick, *Why Johnny Can't Tell Right From Wrong* (New York: Simon and Shuster, 1992).
5. Institute for Research and Evaluation, 6068 S. Jordan Canal Rd., Salt Lake City, UT 84118 (801-966-5644).

Chapter 2

1. Reported in *Newsweek*, February 16, 1987.
2. *Choosing the Best, Student Manual* (Atlanta, GA: 1993).
3. Lou Harris, *op. cit.*
4. "The Games Teenagers Play," *Newsweek*, September 1, 1980.
5. Taken from Coleen Kelly Mast, *Sex Respect: The Option of True Sexual Freedom: A Public Health Workbook for Students.* (Bradley, IL: Respect Incorporated P.O. Box 349, Bradley, Il 60915-0349).
6. National Research Council, *Risking the Future*, (Washington D.C.: National Academy Press, 1987).
7. Mary Patricia Barth Forqurean, "Chastity as Shared Strength: An Open Letter to Students," *America*, November 6, 1993.

Chapter 3

1. Adapted from *No Is A Love Word* (Steubenville, OH: The Human Life Center, 1982).

2. You can order a copy of this tape (which we highly recommend for young people, both for its content and humor) and a list of books on relationships by Dick Purnell, by writing to: Dick Purnell Ministry, P.O. Box 850846, Richardson, TX 75085 (214-234-0855).

3. Dick Purnell, *Becoming a Friend and Lover* (San Bernardino, CA: Here's Life Publishers, 1986).

Part 2

1. "Love Waits" (Falls Christian Action Council: 101 Broad St., Suite 500, Falls Church, VA 22046).

Chapter 4

1. Source: National Center for Health Statistics.

2. "Children Having Children," *Time*, December 9, 1985.

3. J.A. Richardson and G. Dixon, "Effects of legal termination on a subsequent pregnancy," *British Medical Journal*, pp. 1303-04, 1976.

4. Adapted from "Women Form WEBA to Fight Abortions," *Washington Times*, August 3, 1983.

5. "Abortion: Healing the Spiritual Trauma," *New Covenant*, July/August, 1989.

Chapter 5

1. H.M. Bauer, et. al., "Genital human papillomavirus infection in female university students," *JAMA* 265:472-477, 1991.

2. W.J. Kassler and W. Cates Jr., "The epidemiology and prevention of sexually transmitted diseases," Division of STD HIV prevention, Centers for Disease Control, Atlanta, GA, Urologic Clinics of North America, February, 19, 1992.

3. R.E. Johnson, et. al., "A seroepidemiologic survey of the prevalence of herpes simplex 2 infection in the United States," *New England Journal of Medicine* 321: 7-12, 1989.

4. Joe S. McIlhaney, M.D., *Why Condoms Aren't Safe* (Colorado Springs, CO: Focus on the Family, 1993).

Chapter 6

1. "Some Teens Taking Vows of Virginity," *Washington Post*, November 21, 1993.

2. Josh McDowell and Dick Day, *Why Wait: What You Need to Know About the Teen Sexuality Crisis* (San Bernardino, CA: Here's Life Publishers, 1987).

3. *Ibid.*

4. Bob Bartlett, "Going All the Way," *Momentum*, April/May, 1993.

5. Abridged from Ann Landers, "A Not-So-Sweet-Sexteen Story," *Daily News*, September 23, 1991.

6. George B. Eager, *Love, Dating, and Sex* (Valdosta, GA: Mailbox Club Books, 1989).

7. McDowell and Day, *op. cit.*

8. "Safe Sex" (slide show/lecture), Medical Institute for Sexual Health (Austin, TX: 1992).

9. McDowell and Day, *op. cit.*

10. *Choosing the Best, op. cit.*

11. Kieran Sawyer, *Sex and the Teenager: Choice and Decisions* (Notre Dame: Ave Maria Press: 1990).

12. McDowell and Day, *op. cit.*

13. Ann Landers, "Despite Urgin, He's a Virgin," *Daily News*, January 22, 1994.

14. Kieran Sawyer, *op. cit.*

15. McDowell and Day, *op. cit.*

16. *Ibid.*

17. "Everyday Ethical Choices," *Psychology Today*, November, 1981.

18. Howard and Martha Lewis, *The Parent's Guide to Teenage Sex and Pregnancy* (New York: St. Martin's Press, 1980).

Part 3

1. Jane Gross, "Sex Educators for Young See New Virtue in Chastity," *New York Times*, January 16, 1994.

2. Nancy Gibbs, "How Should We Teach Our Children About Sex?" *Time*, May 24, 1993.

3. *Ibid.*

4. *Ibid.*

Chapter 7

1. Adapted from Joseph S. McIlhaney, Jr., M.D., *Why Condoms Aren't Safe* (Colorado Springs, CO: Focus on the Family, 1993).

2. Gibbs, *op. cit.*

3. E. Jones and J. Forrest, "Contraceptive failure in the United States," *Family Planning Perspectives*, May/June, 1989.

4. *Social Science and Medicine*, Vol. 36, 1993.

5. R. Gordon and N. Bjorklund, "If semen were red: the flow of red dye from the tips of condoms during intercourse and its consequences for the AIDS epidemic," paper presented at the WHO Conference Assessing AIDS Prevention, Montreaux, Switzerland, October, 1990.

6. "Condoms: Experts Fear False Sense of Security," *The New York Times*, August 18, 1987.

7. Russell Shaw, "Condom 'Cure' Questioned by Top AIDS Researcher," *Our Sunday Visitor*, January 23, 1994.

8. W. Andre Lafrance, M.D., *The Deadly Con Game*, 1992.

9. "Condoms: Experts Fear False Sense of Security," *The New York Times*, August 18, 1987.

10. Taken from testimony before the United States House of Representatives Subcommittee on Health and Environment, February 10, 1987.

Chapter 8

1. Patricia Driscoll, *Sex Appreciation: A Handbook on Chastity* (Pleasant Hill, CA: Womanity, 1988).

2. Julia Duin, *Purity Makes the Heart Grow Stronger: Sexuality and the Single Christian* (Ann Arbor, MI: Vine Books, 1988).

3. *Human Sexuality: A Catholic Perspective for Education and Lifelong Learning* (Washington D.C.: United States Catholic Conference, 1990).

4. Dick Purnell, *Becoming A Friend and Lover* (San Bernadino, CA: Here's Life Publishers, 1986).

5. Kieran Sawyer, *Sex and the Teenager: Choices and Decisions* (Notre Dame, IN: Ave Maria Press, 1990).

Chapter 10

1. Kathleen Galvin and Bernard Brommel, *Family Communication* (Glenview, IL: Scott, Foresman, and Co., 1986).

2. These studies are reviewed in the book *The Pursuit of Happiness* by David G. Myers.

3. These and subsequent excerpts are taken from Laura Schlessinger's article, "The Cohabitation Trap," *Cosmopolitan*, March, 1994.

Chapter 11

1. Pat Driscoll, "What Is Wrong With Sex Outside Marriage?" (pamphlet available from Womanity, 1700 Oak Park Blvd. Annex, Pleasant Hill, CA 94523).

2. McDowell and Day, *op. cit.*

3. "Report on Sexual Harassment," American Association of University Women, June, 1993 (summarized in *Harvard Education Letter*, Summer, 1993).

Chapter 12

1. Reported in *Family Planning Perspectives*, March/April, 1993.

Chapter 13

1. Coleen Kelly Mast, *op. cit.*

2. George Eager, *Love, Dating, and Sex* (Valdosta, GA: Mailbox Club Books, 1989).

3. Thomas Lorimer, *Why Not? Why Is Premarital Sex Wrong?* (Chattanooga, TN: AMG Publishers, 1993).

4. *Ibid.*

5. "Dear Abby," *Chicago Tribune*, New York News Syndicate, 1968.

Part 4

1. Quotes taken from the videotape, "Love and Life" (which introduces the Christian version of the *Sex Respect* course), *op. cit.*

Chapter 14

1. Reported in *The Bible Today*, September, 1987.

2. *A Community of Caring, op. cit.*, p. 412-413.

3. *Ibid.*, p. 414.

4. *Ibid.*, pp. 416-417.

Chapter 15

1. Pat Driscoll, "God's Plan for Sex" (pamphlet available from Womanity, 1700 Oak Park Blvd. Annex, Pleasant Hill, CA 94523).

2. "Some Teens Taking Vows of Virginity," *Washington Post*, November 21, 1993.

3. Coleen Kelly Mast, *op. cit.*

Chapter 16

1. Coleen Kelly Mast, *op. cit.*

2. Molly Kelly, *Let's Talk to Teens About Chastity* (Villa Maria, PA: The Center for Learning, 1991).

3. Greg Speck, *Sex: It's Worth Waiting For* (Chicago, IL: Moody Press, 1989).

4. *Ibid.*

5. Thomas Lorimer, *op. cit.*

6. Josh McDowell and Dick Day, *op. cit.*

7. *Ibid.*

8. Pat Driscoll, *op. cit.*

Chapter 17

1. Reported in *South Bend Tribune*, December 19, 1993.

2. John and Cathy Colligan, *The Healing Power of Love* (Mahwah, NJ: Paulist Press, 1988).